MW00902025

# Other Books by Stanley Turkel

*Heroes of the American Reconstruction* (2005)

*Great American Hoteliers: Pioneers of the Hotel Industry* (2009)

*Built to Last: 100+ Year-Old Hotels in New York* (2011)

*Built to Last: 100+ Year-Old Hotels East of the Mississippi* (2013)

*Hotel Mavens: Lucius M. Boomer, George C. Boldt and Oscar of the Waldorf* (2014)

*Great American Hoteliers Volume 2: Pioneers of the Hotel Industry* (2016)

*Built to Last: 100+ Year-Old Hotels West of the Mississippi* (2017)

*Hotel Mavens Volume 2: Henry Morrison Flagler, Henry Bradley Plant, Carl Graham Fisher* (2018)

*Great American Hotel Architects Volume 1* (2019)

*Hotel Mavens Volume 3: Bob and Larry Tisch, Curt Strand, Ralph Hitz, Cesar Ritz, Raymond Orteig* (2020)

# GREAT AMERICAN HOTEL ARCHITECTS

## VOLUME 2

STANLEY TURKEL, CMHS

**author**HOUSE®

*AuthorHouse™*
*1663 Liberty Drive*
*Bloomington, IN 47403*
*www.authorhouse.com*
*Phone: 833-262-8899*

*Published by AuthorHouse 10/27/2020*

*ISBN: 978-1-6655-0253-5 (sc)*
*ISBN: 978-1-6655-0251-1 (hc)*
*ISBN: 978-1-6655-0252-8 (e)*

*Library of Congress Control Number: 2019903978*

*Print information available on the last page.*

# DEDICATION

To my son, Marc Alexander Turkel, whose high intelligence and good humor have led to a remarkable life:

- played the violin in Carnegie Hall when he graduated from New York's Music and Art High School
- made the dean's list at Rochester Institute of Technology's Eastman Kodak School of Photography
- recruited by the Microsoft Corporation
- served as a seminar leader at the Landmark Forum
- has been accepted at Seattle University for a master's degree in Existential Phenomenological Psychology

To my daughter, Allison Lee Turkel, whose brilliance and hard work have led to an achievement-filled life:

- graduated from Bronx High School of Science with eight major letters in three varsity sports
- earned a four-year scholarship to the University of Pennsylvania
- made the dean's list at Temple University Law School
- worked for nine years as an assistant district attorney in the Manhattan District Attorney's Office
- was selected to attend the Federal Executive Institute at the US Department of Justice

# CONTENTS

# INTRODUCTION

In the post-Civil War period, real estate developers create a new style of housing for affluent families. The apartment hotel was designed on the European plan for families to live separately in their different suites of apartments without individual kitchens. Meals were served in restaurant-type dining rooms catering exclusively to residents. The apartment hotels employed full-time service staffs, provided ground floor restaurants, and served daily room service meals.

The first apartment hotels were built between 1880 and 1895. They were followed by a second wave of construction after the passage of the 1899 building code and the 1901 Tenement House Law. The third wave of apartment hotel construction occurred during the 1920s and ended with the Great Depression of the thirties. The passage of the Multiple Dwelling Act of 1929 altered height and bulk restrictions and permitted high-rise apartment buildings for the first time.

Here, in summary, are the 304 hotels and apartment hotels designed by the fourteen architects described in this study of *Great American Hotel Architects Volume 2*:

J. E. R. Carpenter

- Hermitage Hotel, Nashville, Tennessee
- forty-six apartment hotels in New York, New York

Rosario Candela

- eighty-one apartment hotels in New York, New York

Harrison Albright

- Richmond Hotel, Richmond, Virginia
- West Baden Springs Hotel, West Baden, Indiana
- U. S. Grant Hotel, San Diego, California
- Golden West Hotel, San Diego, California

Hiss & Weekes

- Gotham Hotel, New York, New York
- Belnord Apartments, New York, New York

Schwartz & Gross

- Hotel Lincoln, New York, New York
- seventy-nine apartment hotels in New York, New York

Sugarman & Berger

- New Yorker Hotel, New York, New York
- One Fifth Avenue, New York, New York
- Gramercy Arms, New York, New York
- Hotel Paris, New York, New York
- Navarro Flats, New York, New York

Frank Mills Andrews

- Hotel McAlpin, New York, New York
- George Washington Hotel, New York, New York
- Hotel Taft, New Haven, Connecticut

Murgatroyd & Ogden

- Allerton House, New York, New York
- Allerton House, Cleveland, Ohio
- Allerton House, Chicago, Illinois
- Barbizon Hotel for Women, New York, New York
- Hotel Governor Clinton, New York, New York
- Barbizon Plaza Hotel, New York, New York

Paul Revere Williams

- Twenty-Eighth Street YMCA, Los Angeles, California
- Hollywood YMCA, Hollywood, California
- Hotel Nutibara, Medellin, Colombia
- Knickerbocker Hotel, Hollywood, California
- Beverly Hills Hotel, Beverly Hills, California
- Hotel Granada, Bogotá, Colombia
- La Concha Motel, Las Vegas, Nevada

Holabird & Roche

- The University Club of Chicago, Chicago, Illinois
- Hotel Muehlebach, Kansas City, Missouri
- The Nicollet Hotel, Minneapolis, Minnesota
- The Palmer House, Chicago, Illinois
- Stevens Hotel, Chicago, Illinois

John C. Portman Jr.

- Hyatt Regency Hotel, Atlanta, Georgia
- Hyatt Regency O'Hare Hotel, Rosemont, Georgia
- Hyatt Regency Hotel, San Francisco, California
- Le Meridian Hotel, San Francisco, California

- Hyatt Regency Hotel, Houston, Texas
- Westin Peachtree Plaza Hotel, Atlanta, Georgia
- Westin Bonaventure Hotel, Los Angeles, California
- Marriott Hotel at Renaissance Center, Detroit, Michigan
- The Regent Hotel, Singapore
- Marriott Marquis Hotel, Atlanta, Georgia
- Pan Pacific Hotel, Singapore
- Marriott Marquis Hotel, New York, New York
- JW Marriott Union Square Hotel, San Francisco, California
- The Portman Ritz-Carlton, Singapore
- Westin Bundt Center Hotel, Singapore
- Westin Warsaw Hotel, Warsaw, Poland
- Westin Charlotte Hotel, Charlotte, North Carolina
- Renaissance Convention Center Hotel, Schaumberg, Illinois
- Hilton Bayfront Hotel, San Diego, California

Henry Hohauser

- Park Central Hotel, Miami Beach, Florida
- The Colony Hotel, Miami Beach, Florida
- Edison Hotel, Miami Beach, Florida
- Essex House Hotel, Miami Beach, Florida
- Cardoza Hotel, Miami Beach, Florida
- Crescent Hotel, Miami Beach, Florida
- The Novick Hotel, Miami Beach, Florida
- The Century Hotel, Miami Beach, Florida
- The Davis Hotel, Miami Beach, Florida
- Collins Plaza Hotel, Miami Beach, Florida
- Collins Park Hotel, Miami Beach, Florida
- Neron Hotel, Miami Beach, Florida

- The Parc Vendome Hotel, Miami Beach, Florida
- The Greystone Hotel, South Beach, Florida

Dorothy Draper

- Carlyle Hotel, New York, New York
- Sherry-Netherland Hotel, New York, New York
- Drake Hotel, Chicago, Illinois
- Fairmont Hotel, San Francisco, California
- Hampshire House Hotel, New York, New York
- The Greenbrier Hotel, White Sulphur Springs
- St. Anthony Hotel, San Antonio, Texas, West Virginia
- Arrowhead Springs Resort, San Bernardino, California

Morris Lapidus

- Grossinger's Catskill Resort Hotel, Fallsburg, New York
- Fontainebleau Hotel, Miami Beach, Florida
- Eden Roc Hotel, Miami Beach, Florida
- Aruba Hotel, Aruba
- Americana of Bal Harbour, Miami Beach, Florida
- Deauville Resort, Miami Beach, Florida
- Concord Resort Hotel, Fallsburg, New York
- Golden Triangle Motor Hotel, Norfolk, Virginia
- Sheraton Motor Inn, New York, New York
- The Summit Hotel, New York, New York
- Ponce de Leon Hotel, San Juan, Puerto Rico
- Richmond Motel, Richmond, Virginia
- The Americana of New York, New York, New York
- The Americana of San Juan, San Juan, Puerto Rico
- International Inn, Washington, DC
- Capitol Skyline Hotel, Washington, DC

- El Conquistador Resort, Fajardo, Puerto Rico
- San Juan Intercontinental Hotel, San Juan, Puerto Rico
- Portman Square Hotel, London, England
- The Tropicana, Sunny Isles Beach, Florida

# FOREWORD

Stanley Turkel, the unofficial, but widely recognized as the greatest hotel historian, is at it again with *Great American Hotel Architects Volume 2*. Stan's prolific writings include ten books and hundreds of articles dedicated to keeping hotel history alive so we all can hopefully learn from the past.

His newest work recognizes fourteen hotel architects spanning more than 120 years of hotel history in the United States. Stan's book documents the achievements of these great designers and provides a glimpse into what actually happens inside their hotels. Readers will learn about the trials and tribulations involved with getting a hotel built, what famous guests frequented the properties, the trail of ownership changes, and what the hotels are doing today. Many of the hotels set records for the tallest, the largest, or the first with an elevator; one even started as a brothel (some architects will work on anything).

The book provides clues about Stan's background and the source of his wealth of knowledge with his informative notes throughout. He was the resident manager or general manager of many hotels. You cannot write a book crammed full of detailed hotel operational information without actually living in a hotel like Stan has done throughout his professional career.

As a hotel appraiser, I find one of the most important valuation considerations is the hotel's useful life. The average economic life of a hotel is forty years with a standard deviation of twenty years. This means an owner needs to build the hotel, operate the hotel, periodically renovate and refurbish the hotel, and get all their invested dollars back during a life that could be as short as twenty years or as long as sixty years. An important component that determines the economic life of a hotel is its physical design, which is largely the responsibility of the architect. And we are not only talking about the exterior façade, but also the access and visibility, the placement on the site, and the sense of arrival.

One of the most important responsibilities of the architect that guests seldom focus on is the layout and design of interior spaces. Hotels are complex businesses that provide guest rooms lobbies, restaurants, bars, lounges, fitness centers, meeting rooms, and banquet rooms. These spaces need to work together to support the flow of guests and hotel personnel. In addition, a hotel has a back of the house: kitchens, receiving, storage, laundry, mechanical systems, maintenance areas, executive offices, accounting departments, and the list goes on.

Hotel architects are basically designing a city, and for a hotel to be economically viable, all these spaces and businesses need to work and function together—and it's the architect who makes it happen. Successful hotel architects must know how to design a pretty building and understand how a hotel works. It's a real specialty. Many of the hotels featured in Stan's book achieved an economic life of more than sixty years.

Stan provides a wonderful description of the complexities of designing a world-class hotel with his inventory of what went into the New Yorker Hotel (Manhattan's largest and tallest hotel in 1929), which was designed by Sugarman & Berger:

- a "vertical city"
- front desk with twenty clerks
- restaurants with world-famous orchestras
- walls of Persian walnut inlaid with solid brass
- kitchens covering an acre of floor space with 135 of the world's famous cooks
- twenty-three elevators, speeding at eight hundred feet per minute
- bedrooms with Servidors, circulating ice water, hand telephones, bed-head, reading lamps, full-length mirrors, and full-sized beds
- largest barber shop in the world: forty-two chairs and twenty manicurists
- largest private power plant in the world
- a ten-room hospital

This is why Stanley Turkel wrote a book about these largely unsung heroes of the hotel industry. His book provides important recognition of the architects who can directly impact the overall long-term success of a hotel. When you arrive at a hotel, you recognize it is a Hilton, Marriott, Hyatt, etc., but do you know who the architect was? I am glad Stan is now giving the great hotel architects the recognition they rightly deserved.

Steve Rushmore
Founder, HVS

# Chapter 1

## Apartment Hotels

In October 1866, the *New York Times* reported that most middle-class families who were too affluent for tenement houses could not afford to lease a townhouse for their own use. While top society looked down on hotel living, it did not have the stigma of boardinghouse life. While more expensive, hotel living was popular with families who saw the "apartment hotel" as a form of cooperative housing to resolve the middle-class housing dilemma. By 1869, there were between two hundred and eight hundred hotels catering to long-term residents.

In 1870, a year after the completion of Richard Morris Hunt's Stuyvesant Apartments, David and Richard Haight commissioned architect Stephen D. Hatch to rebuild their former mansion at Fifth Avenue and Fifteenth Street. Hatch converted it into a five-story multiple dwelling with five apartments per floor and an Otis elevator. While there was a large common dining room, each apartment also had its own smaller dining room. Residents could order through the steward to have meals prepared in the common kitchen and served in their own rooms. Haight House also provided a central steam laundry and a porter who monitored the comings and goings of tenants and their guests. Some of these apartments were more luxurious than those at other apartment hotels, with some dining rooms large enough to seat eighteen people and lavishly appointed master bathrooms. On the top floor, bachelors were accommodated in two- and three-room apartments.

While Haight House combined features of an apartment house with a hotel, Detlef Lienau's Grosvenor House at Fifth Avenue and Tenth Street was New York's first purpose-built apartment hotel. Richardson called the building "a success from the start … with a singularly clean conception of the wants of a particular class of New York families—a class possessing wealth, culture, refinement and love of ease." The Grosvenor was an L-shaped structure wrapped around a forty-foot courtyard.

Richard Morris Hunt's six-story Stevens House at Fifth Avenue and Twenty-Seventh Street was a superb work of architecture with eighteen apartments. It was commissioned by Paran Stevens, "the Napoleon of Hotel Keepers," who operated hotels in various cities including the Fifth Avenue Hotel in New York. The Stevens House was designed on the European plan for families to live separately in their different suites of apartments. Hunt eliminated the individual apartment kitchens in favor of a restaurant-type dining room catering exclusively to residents, thereby establishing an apartment hotel. In 1879, it was renovated again as the Victoria Hotel with five hundred transient rooms.

In April 1853, *Putnam Magazine* reported: "Society is rapidly tending towards hotel life and the advantages of a cluster of families living together under one roof are everyday more apparent."

Developer Amos R. Eno built the five-hundred-room, six-story white-marble Fifth Avenue Hotel at Fifth Avenue and Twenty-Third Street. At first known as "Eno's Folly," the location was mocked as too far uptown "living among the goats." The Fifth Avenue Hotel was followed by the Albemarle Hotel by architects Renwick & Auchmutz in 1860 and in 1864 by John B. Snook's Hoffman House at Twenty-Fifth Street and Broadway.

Next came the Grand Hotel by Henry Englehart in 1868, far uptown at Thirty-First Street. Critic Montgomery Schuyler reported that the Grand Hotel "loomed up with immense proportions in [its] neighborhood until its larger rival—the Gilsey—came to overtop it … [forming] the present northern boundary of colossal hotels, almost of architectural improvements."

Hatch's Gilsey House, built by the Danish-born real estate developer and politician Peter Gilsey, contained three hundred rooms and was rendered in cast iron and painted white to imitate marble. Montgomery Schuyler wrote, "While open to the objections that all iron buildings … profess an imitation of stone workmanship, it is certainly one of the finest of this class in the city."

Hotel life was seen as a solution for working women as well. In the 1860s, the Working Women's House was created in a rehabilitated tenement building at 45 Elizabeth Street with five hundred beds in curtained alcoves as well as parlors, a reading room, a laundry, and a common dining room. Alexander T. Stewart, who employed many single women in his wholesale and retail stores, built a "hotel for women of modest means" between Thirty-Second and Thirty-Third Streets. Designed by architect John Kellum, the Working Women's Hotel opened in 1878 with five hundred well-furnished bedrooms around an interior courtyard. According to the *American Architect and Building News*, each bedroom "[is] finished in good style, and each room has hot and cold water taps, gas and electric, bell communication with the office. Bathrooms and water closets are provided in abundance." The street level was lined with shops while the upper floors afforded many features of a first-class hotel, including parlors, reading rooms, a six-hundred-seat dining room, and a concert and assembly room. Elevators connected all seven floors.

Alexander Stewart died two years before his Working Women's Hotel opened. His executor closed the building down fifty-three days after its opening. After minor renovations, the building reopened as the Park Avenue Hotel, catering to an entirely different market.

An editorial in the *New York Times* (June 3, 1878) titled "A Revolution in Living" stated:

> Within a few years a change in the way of living has been made here but the change has been so quiet and gradual as to excite almost no public attention. In a very short time, indeed, this City may be said to have entered on what may be called a domiciliary revolution. The revolution has no more fairly begun, but it is rapidly spreading, and will before long become complete. It has already been of much benefit to the community, and the benefit will continually increase, since it adds materially to the convenience, comfort, and wholesomeness of our homes. The desirable change is in the substitution of flats or apartment houses, as they are generally named here, for boarding houses, and the entire or partial occupation of dwellings.

During the 1880s, apartment hotels catered to well-to-do families who began to relocate to New York City. These hotels provided suites of rooms that were serviced by the hotel staff, thereby eliminating the need for servants. By 1905, it was estimated that there were almost one hundred such hotels in midtown Manhattan. Apartment hotels were designed to house both transient guests and permanent tenants in single rooms and suites, furnished or unfurnished. Most were without kitchen facilities. Instead, the hotels employed full-time service staffs, provided ground-floor restaurants, and served extensive room service meals throughout.

The first wave of these apartment hotels was built between 1880 and 1895. A second wave of construction followed the passage of the new building code in 1899 and the Tenement House Law in 1901. Since apartment hotels were classified as hotels rather than regular apartment buildings, they were exempt from the more stringent tenement housing law and regulated only by the more flexible building code as applied to commercial buildings. As a consequence, apartment hotels could be less fireproof, taller, cover a larger portion of the lot, and contain more units than apartment houses, giving builders a larger financial return.

The third wave of apartment hotel construction during the prosperity of the 1920s ended with the Great Depression of the thirties. The passage of the Multiple Dwelling Act of 1929 altered height and bulk restrictions and permitted high-rise apartment buildings for the first time. This law, combined with the Great Depression, effectively ended the development of apartment hotels.

Some apartment hotels introduced "bootleg kitchens" into their suites, intended for warming up food prepared by room service. Under the law, which was not strictly enforced, stoves were still not allowed in living units of apartment hotels. Many were illegally retrofitted in this manner.

In 1887, the architects and builders Hubert, Pirsson, and Company proposed an apartment hotel to be built on the site of the original Madison Square Garden (which was built instead to McKim, Mead, & White's design). This pioneering design was to consist of "small two-story houses each twenty-two by fifty feet, and set one on top of another." These 240 "houses" would have been connected at their parlor levels by fourteen-foot-wide "aerial sidewalks" cantilevered beyond the building line by four feet. Pairs of elevators at each of the four corners of the building were to provide vertical circulation for tenants and guests, while dumbwaiters situated between each pair of apartments would have handled deliveries and garbage removal.

While this unique apartment hotel never was built, Hubert introduced the duplex apartment unit in the cooperatively financed and maintained Hubert Home Clubs. Philip Gengembre Hubert, a French-American, used his mother's maiden name upon emigrating to the United States. He was a broad-based, creative man who financed his architectural studies with the income from his many patents, one of which was for the first self-fastening button, which he sold to the US Army. Hubert formed a partnership with James L. Pirsson, and together they created the cooperative experiment known as the Hubert Home Clubs. Their first project was the Rembrandt, a Home Club for artists on West Fifty-Seventh Street adjacent to the yet-to-be built Carnegie Hall.

In *New York, New York: How the Apartment House Transformed the Life of the City (1869–1930)* Elizabeth Hawes writes,

> To the members of a Home Club, Hubert, Pirsson and Company proposed sharing far more than the controversial common roof. Under the terms of a

cooperative home association, as it was formally known, tenants—"a number of gentlemen of congenial tastes, and occupying the same social positions in life"—formed a club, or joint stock company, to share the cost of land and a building, with each associate receiving a proprietary lease on a suite appropriate to his investment, and with an excess of suites to be rented to pay the mortgage and running expenses. Soon after the appearance of the Rembrandt, for example, a group of eight families projected a building of six stories on three lots; it would translate into apartments of 2,200 square feet; reception room, library, dining room, hallway, three bedchambers, kitchen, servant's rooms and drying rooms on the top floor. In addition, adjacent to this apartment house, which was only 56 feet wide, a small four-story English-basement house was to be constructed as a rental property, to supply the funds to pay for a janitor, a fireman, three elevator youths, one hall boy, property and water taxes, repairs, and the maintenance of the front walk.

In concept, Hubert Home Clubs were designed for the wealthy. Hubert had learned from experience that people of limited means could not enter into an arrangement that called for assets and economic risks. His first building, a plain but substantial structure, had been planned for the moderate middle classes, but it filled with well-to-do entrepreneurs. Beginning with the Rembrandt, Hubert recognized the cooperative scheme as an opportunity to create fine, increasingly large, and extravagant apartment buildings.

Hubert Home Cooperative Clubs, therefore, were regarded as suitable replacements for private houses. Hubert was an enthusiastic supporter of the economist Henry George who challenged the accepted economic theory with his best-selling book *Progress and Poverty* in 1879. Hubert's designs for cooperative apartment buildings included many new ideas:

- the first fireproof plaster blocks to reduce the chance of fire
- a self-propelling elevator
- cold-air boxes to preserve food
- a fireproof mansard roof
- a summer roof garden where fountains and sprinklers kept tiles cool
- a device for burning vegetable refuse
- bedsteads that were designed with steam pipes in place of slats, which were connected to steam coils for heat
- bulk purchases of ice and coal to save money for tenants

Hubert's Chelsea Hotel on West Twenty-Third Street built in 1885 is a twelve-story bearing-wall structure that has been called Victorian Gothic, but its style is hard to define. It was the tallest building in New York until 1899. The most prominent exterior features are the delicate floral filigree iron balconies from the foundry of the Cornell Brothers on Center Street. The Chelsea was elaborately designed with gables, dormers, and wide red brick chimneys. Inside, the chosen materials were polished hardwood floors and doors, marble, and onyx. The original Chelsea had a barbershop, restaurant, maid service, artists' studios, a large roof garden, and one hundred apartments—seventy owned by cooperators and thirty rented out. Evening concerts were held in the summer in the fireproofed roof garden. The apartments were large (from three to twelve rooms) and decorated according to the desires of the individual tenants. Servants' quarters were available, but few apartments had full kitchens.

Christopher Gray, the eminent architectural historian wrote in his *New York Times Streetscapes* column (February 15, 1998):

> In 1885, the *Real Estate Record and Guide* said that many of the apartments were owned by tradesmen and suppliers on the project "who were persuaded" to take them in lieu of money—apparently under duress ... The bloom of the co-op movement wilted in 1885 as several failed, and new legislation severely restricted construction of tall apartment houses ... Around 1900 the building began to sift toward transient occupancy—the writer O'Henry stayed there for a short time in 1907. In 1912, Titanic survivors with second-class tickets stayed at the Chelsea for a few days.

Two other examples of the courtyard apartment house were built not for the poor but for the rich. Harde and Short's Alwyn Court (1908) and McKim, Mead, & White's 998 Fifth Avenue (1912) both had such small courts that they were tenements as much as courtyard apartment houses. Yet each was finely detailed, designed to meet a demand for a new type of apartment house in fashionable neighborhoods. As the *Real Estate Record and Guide* commented,

> We must learn to take a very large view of New York, for it is to be the foremost city of the world. The leading families in America are adopting a standard of living which includes more than one home. There is a country home and also a city home. The real homestead is in the country. There's

where the family's treasures are. For the city home, apartments are coming to be preferred over the private dwelling, for one reason, because of private dwelling may not be obtainable in the particular neighborhood where the family wishes to reside in town. The really high-class apartment offers to tenants of wealth and standing the choice of the finest locations in Swelldom.

In 1918, architect George Mort Pollard designed the Hotel des Artistes reminiscent of an Elizabethan manor house with a rich limestone base and carved figures representing the arts. Most of the apartments had English Renaissance paneling in the living and dining rooms. However, there were no kitchens because food was prepared in a central kitchen connected to the apartments by electric dumbwaiters. Although the Hotel des Artistes with its Gothic-style façade is often considered the cornerstone building on a block of artists' studios, it was actually the fifth on the street to be built.

West Sixty-Seventh Street off Central Park West was a street of stables and light industry in 1903, when the first studio building went up at No. 27. There, a syndicate of artists built their own co-op on the north side of the street. Facing the back were double-height studio spaces with the traditional artists' northern light; smaller single-height rooms faced the front. What started as an idea became a movement, and by 1915, the street had been transformed into an artists' haven, with four tall co-ops of varying designs.

That was the year the painter Penrhyn Stanlaws, living in the second studio building, at 33 West Sixty-Seventh, organized a syndicate to build the biggest building yet, taking the address 1

West Sixty-Seventh Street and the name Hotel des Artistes. It was built as a co-op, but it also had rental units.

Despite its name, it was a building not just about art. Stanlaws said that the ten-floor $1.2 million structure was the largest studio building in the world. It had a swimming pool, a squash court, a sun parlor, a ballroom, a first-floor grill and, on the second floor, a much larger restaurant.

Although many apartments were customized during construction, the typical floor had eight small studios facing Sixty-Seventh Street and six small and two double-size studios facing the rear.

The Hotel des Artistes was completed in 1917, and the 1920 census captured the building partly full. In the tally of occupations, there were fourteen artists, musicians, or writers, eleven actors or movie executives, and twenty-two stockbrokers, engineers, and other businesspeople. The most frequent occupation listed was household servant—twenty-six in all.

The artistic contingent included Walter Russel, a Paris-trained artist who had studied with Howard Pyle and painted Theodore Roosevelt's children, and who was one of the originators of the studio idea on West Sixty-Seventh. His neighbors included William Cotton, a muralist, who decorated the old Times Square and Selwyn Theaters; Howard Chandler Christy, who did the murals in the present Café des Artistes, which is adjacent to the building's lobby; and Carolyn Wells Houghton, a popular writer of mysteries and humor books, including *The Rubaiyat of a Motor Car.*

The motion-picture side of the building included Alan Crosland, who directed Al Jolson's *Jazz Singer* of 1927, and George Fitzmaurice, who directed Greta Garbo in the 1931 *Mata Hari.*

In 1925, Fitzmaurice had predicted that, since movies were already being shown on Paris-to-London airplanes, they would soon be available in New York subway cars.

Most of the apartments were small, and there were plenty of one-person households. But Aaron Naumburg, a fur dealer, had an expansive top-floor apartment, filled with art and furnishings. He left his collection to the Fogg Art Museum at Harvard, which still displays it in a reproduction of Naumburg's Sixty-Seventh Street studio, though it is primarily used for staff events and receptions and is not usually open to the public. Naumburg's apartment was later owned by the writer Fannie Hurst.

As the Scottish-born Stanlaws was building the Hotel des Artistes, he was also planning other projects. In 1919, he and Pollard organized the studio building at 2 West Sixty-Seventh Street, and had the architects Carrerre and Hastings plan a grandiose hotel-apartment-resort complex in Port Washington, Long Island, which was never built. Stanlaws also directed Adolphe Menjou in the 1922 movie *Singed Wings*, but his most notable accomplishment remained the Hotel des Artistes. He eventually moved to California, where he died in 1957.

A 1950s brochure offered large studio apartments in the Hotel des Artistes for $150 a month and listed as prominent recent tenants Noel Coward, the writer Edna Ferber, and the actress ZaSu Pitts. In 1952, the ballroom was rented to ABC as a television studio.

Now, the Hotel des Artistes has hired a New Jersey engineering firm, JMA Consultants, to prepare specifications for repairs to the lintels and brickwork on the rear and sides of the building. Gerard J. Picaso, the managing agent, said that the board is looking into cleaning the Sixty-Seventh Street façade. Most of that elevation looks like gray brick, but a test cleaning patch shows that it was originally buff, probably to be complementary to the limestone and terra-cotta also on the façade.

# Chapter 2

## J. E. R. Carpenter (1867–1932)

On June 12, 1932, the following obituary appeared in the *New York Times*: "J. E. R. Carpenter, Architect, is Dead." The write-up featured Carpenter's design of the "Lincoln Building and Other Large Structures; Aided Fifth Avenue Change; Brought Test Suit Clearing Way for Tall Buildings Along Central Park; Active at Palm Beach." In a letter to the editor of The *Real Estate Record and Guide* in 1932, Lawrence B. Elliman said that Mr. Carpenter "was the father of the modern large apartment hotel here in New York."

James Edwin Ruthven Carpenter was born in 1867, son of a well-to-do iron manufacturer in the tiny town of Mount Pleasant, Tennessee. His mother, Jane Wilson Carpenter, was from an old Maury County family that once owned Blythwood, one of the county's most cherished antebellum landmarks. Carpenter attended local schools before entering the University of Tennessee in 1885. Shortly afterward, he transferred to the Massachusetts Institute of Technology to study architecture under the renowned Boston architect Henry H. Richardson, who was reputed to be the most talented American architect of the era. After graduation, he attended at the Ecole des Beaux-Arts in Paris and then landed a job at the one of the country's most prestigious architectural firms: McKim, Mead & White.

Carpenter was on his way to establishing a national career as an architect, but following the death of his father, he returned to Tennessee to help support his family. His first job was as a draftsman for the Columbia arsenal that later became the Columbia Military Academy. He subsequently relocated to Nashville where he practiced architecture with the firm of Hodge and Carpenter. He published a book called *Artistic Homes for City and Suburb,* which contained descriptions, floor plans, and sketches for fourteen homes suited to the South. In 1892, Carpenter moved to Norfolk, Virginia, where he started an architectural office with John Kevan Peeples. They designed the Monticello Hotel in Norfolk, the Fayerweather Gymnasium at the University of Virginia, business and commercial buildings, churches, and homes across the state.

After Carpenter returned from the Ecole des Beaux-Arts in Paris, he collaborated to design a number of important buildings in Tennessee, including the St. Thomas Hospital (1903), the Maury County Courthouse (1905), and the rebuilt Main Building at Vanderbilt University (1906). Carpenter designed the sixteen-story Empire Building (1909); the Ridgely Apartments (1914) in Birmingham, Alabama; the American National Bank Building in Pensacola, Florida; and the Hurt Building in Atlanta in 1913. However, it was his well-praised design for the Stahlman Building that secured the commission for Nashville's first million-dollar hotel—the Hermitage Hotel—in 1909.

## The Hermitage Hotel, Nashville, Tennessee

With the growth of Nashville at the end of the nineteenth century, a group of community movers and shakers decided to build Nashville's first million-dollar hotel. They realized that there was a shortage of first-class hotels in the city even with Nashville's other major hotels: the Duncan Hotel, the Maxwell House, and the Tulane Hotel.

In June 1908, nineteen businessmen incorporated the Hermitage Hotel Company with capital of $350,000. Of this amount, $100,000 came from the architect James Edwin Ruthven Carpenter who was said to be the first native Tennessean to be formally trained in architecture. Carpenter teamed with Walter D. Blair who had previously attended Richmond College, the University of Virginia, and the University of Pennsylvania. Carpenter also invited architect Russell Eason Hart to move to Nashville to serve as resident architect during the construction of the Hermitage Hotel.

J. E. R. Carpenter's design for the Hermitage was intended to be equal to the finest in the United States. In 1909, the *Commercial History of the State of Tennessee* provided details about the new hotel's design:

> The decorative effects will be artistic and pleasing. The lobby and all the public rooms on the first floor will be finished in the finest grade of Italian marble with marbled floors, etc. The main dining room walls will be finished in Circassian walnut paneling. The ceiling decorations will be handsome and elaborate in harmony with purposes of the room. The Grill Room is unique; the ceiling being a series of domes, carried on columns.

A caption from the September 18, 1910, edition of the *Nashville Tennessean* read:

> This magnificent new hostelry was opened to the public Saturday night at 6 o'clock. Although all the

fixtures have not been installed, the lobby, parlors, and dining room are completed in the most modern and elegant style. In every particular it will rank as one of the leading and most perfectly furnished hotels in the entire country. Every detail has been worked on for the satisfaction of the most fastidious. The service is par excellence.

When the Hermitage opened in 1910, it advertised its rooms as "fireproof, noise proof and dustproof, $2.00 and up." Each guest room had a private bath, telephone, electric fan, and a device that indicated the arrival of mail. The Hermitage was a symbol of Nashville's emergence as a major southern city. As Nashville's first million-dollar hotel, no expense was spared in its furnishings: sienna marble in the entrance; wall panels of Russian walnut; a stained glass ceiling in the vaulted lobby; Persian rugs and massive overstuffed furniture. Downstairs, adjoining the Oak Bar, was the Grille Room (now the Capitol Grille), which was built by German craftsmen and became a private men's-only club.

The Hermitage has enjoyed a long relationship with the music industry as Nashville became known as Music City and home of the historic Grand Ole Opry. The hotel was the headquarters for the suffragette movement in 1920 as the state of Tennessee cast the deciding ballot in passage of the Nineteenth Amendment, giving women the right to vote. The Hermitage was also the home for eight years of legendary pool player Minnesota "Fats," and the hotel management installed a $3,200 Steepleton billiards table on the mezzanine above the lobby.

One of the longest-serving general managers of the Hermitage was Howard E. Baughman. Highly energetic and able, he managed the hotel from 1929 to 1946 and was remembered by W. D. Brown who ran the hotel barbershop for forty-seven years:

> He was really a hotel man. He was always busy. I would open shop at eight o'clock. At 8:05 every morning he would walk in my door. He had already started at the top and inspected everything hiking all the way down to the basement. There were always a lot of bellboys around in those days. If he started talking to someone in the lobby, he might motion to one of the boys. The bellboy knew what to do. He went to the desk and got the man's name and slipped it to Mr. Baughman, who always liked to call a guest by his name. He was as straight as he could be. He would do anything for a guest. If the hotel was full and a regular guest came in, he would take him to his apartment. Baughman had an apartment on the sixth floor.

For many years, the Hermitage was the center of Nashville's social and political life, hosting everything from formal functions in its grand ballroom to pep rallies for Vanderbilt University's football team. The Meyer Hotel Company leased the hotel from 1918 to 1956.

Robert Randolph Meyer (1882–1947) modeled his hotel company after the Statler Hotels chain. As an experienced hotelier, Meyer was brought in to consult on the opening of Birmingham's Tutwiler Hotel in 1914. Meyer's "Robert Meyer Hotels" management portfolio included the Winecoff Hotel in Atlanta, Georgia; the Hotel Windsor and Hotel Roosevelt in Jacksonville, Florida, the Hotel Stacy-Trent in Trenton, New Jersey; the Abraham Lincoln Hotel in Reading, Pennsylvania; the Hotel Sir Walter in Raleigh,

North Carolina; the Emerson Hotel in Baltimore, Maryland; the Farragut Hotel in Knoxville, Tennessee; and the Hermitage Hotel in Nashville, Tennessee.

In 1969, the Hermitage was sold to the Alsonett Hotels Company, and after years of difficulty and deterioration, they finally shut it down in 1979. The Brock Hotel Corporation, the nation's largest independent operator of Holiday Inns, acquired the hotel, and after an extensive renovation, they reopened it in 1981. However, Brock was not successful, and in 2000, he sold the Hermitage Hotel to Historic Hotels of Nashville whose stated business goal was to gain the AAA Five-Diamond rating. During the multiyear, $17 million renovation and restoration project, architect Ron Gobbell used historic photographs as a guide for the faithful and interpretive restoration.

In the ballroom, where the burbled walnut paneling had dulled after years of deterioration and grime, crews worked tirelessly to remove the dirt and old varnish by hand. Once the wood had been stripped, they hand-applied three new coats of varnish to restore the paneling's lustrous gleam. Throughout the various renovations, one part of the hotel remained virtually untouched: the green and black Art Deco-style men's room in the basement, which was installed in 1910. After renovation and restoration of its original shoeshine stand, the bathroom has become a landmark in its own right, even winning the title of "America's Best Restroom" in an online contest.

The Hermitage Hotel is one of the great hotels in the United States for many reasons, not the least of which is Tom Vickstrom, director of finance, who is also a talented and impassioned hotel historian. His indefatigable research has resulted in a series of newsletters, "Reflections from the Past," which are written for the ever-growing circle of friends and associates who enjoy history and have a special sentimental connection with the Hermitage Hotel. The newsletters are chockfull of vintage photographs; stories about Hermitage guests, famous and infamous; family recollections; great memories; old menus; nostalgic wedding pictures; former employees; and Hermitage Hotel memorabilia.

The Hermitage Hotel was listed on the National Register of Historic Places in 1975. It is Tennessee's only AAA Five-Diamond and Forbes Travel Guide Five-Star Award hotel.

Carpenter was hired to design a new apartment hotel in New York City. That original apartment building was called the Fullerton, and Carpenter made one of the apartments his own home. He also invested in the building, which distinguished him from Rosario Candela for the rest of his career. Now demolished, the building had a white terra-cotta façade in the Renaissance style.

Two years later, the Fullerton-Weaver Company with Carpenter as the architect, built the singular 960 Park Avenue at Eighty-Second Street, which has stood for more than one hundred years as a model for luxurious apartment buildings.

Carpenter is credited with the initiation and perfection of the "off-the-foyer" apartment layout, although he acknowledged that the first steps in that direction were taken by the architect William Alciphron Boring (1859–1931) in his plans for 520 and 540 Park Avenue. Carpenter knew Boring from his days at the Ecole des Beaux-Arts in Paris. Boring also designed the Ellis Island immigration center in 1895 and became dean at the Columbia University School of Architecture.

In 1916, Carpenter designed 907 Fifth Avenue with simplexes and grand duplexes, one with five bedrooms, a twenty-by-thirty-foot living room and a forty-seven-foot-long gallery. He was also an investor in this building and occupied an apartment. Carpenter continued with architectural projects on Fifth Avenue along Central Park until January 1922 when the city restricted the heights to seventy-five feet until Carpenter brought the test case that overturned the restriction in 1923. A flood of new construction followed within the next years with more than a dozen buildings designed by J. E. R. Carpenter. One distinctive aspect of Carpenter's designs was his pairing of buildings that faced each other across a side street.

In 1919, the *Architecture Forum* published a long article about Carpenter's projects describing his role in both the design and business parts of the projects:

> Success has topped it all—success for the investors, for the architect, and for the tenant. In fact, with no failures charged against him, Mr. Carpenter stands as an unquestioned authority on this special phase of building development, it being the general custom of realty and financial men in the metropolis to first submit for his review any/such projected improvement of property.

A 1930 ad in the *New York Times* for several of his apartment buildings noted, "there is a quiet restful feeling about these apartments in their large, high ceiling rooms, the careful finish of detail, the skilled but unobtrusive service."

When Carpenter died suddenly in 1932, the following letter by Lawrence Elliman of Pease and Elliman appeared in the *Real Estate Record and Guide*:

> In the sudden death of J. Edwin R. Carpenter, the real estate fraternity has lost a real friend and a man who, through breadth of vision and initiative, probably had more to do with the development of the modern apartment houses than any other single man. Mr. Carpenter brought to this field of activity a technical training and an intimate knowledge of what the better class of New Yorker required in the way of housing. Through his intuitive knowledge of how people wish to live he developed a type of apartment that had not heretofore existed. His first outstanding success was at 116 West 58th Street in which was shown for the first time a new type, consisting of an entrance gallery instead of the old fashioned foyer hall. This idea was further extended in his next building at 960 Park Avenue, and was probably best exemplified in his building at 630 Park Avenue, which is generally considered the finest plan that has ever been developed here in New York. His new idea of apartment construction has been largely copied in practically all of the modern construction; so I think it fair to state that Mr. Carpenter is the father of the modern large apartment here in New York. Mr. Carpenter has been a very powerful factor for the last 25 years in modern housing of all types here in New York, and his passing marks the end of an extraordinary era of high-class apartments.

# Chronology of Carpenter New York Apartment Houses

| Address | Filed | Begun | Completed |
|---|---|---|---|
| 116 East 58th Street (demolished) | 07-24-09 | ---- | 09-27-10 |
| 960 Park Avenue | 06-09-11 | 09-26-11 | 08-06-12 |
| 246 West End Avenue | 08-16-12 | 08-25-12 | 06-24-13 |
| 3 East 85th Street | 1912 | ---- | 12-04-13 |
| 635 Park Avenue | 10-29-12 | 12-24-12 | 10-31-14 |
| 640 Park Avenue | 1913 | 11-14-13 | 08-15-14 |
| 907 Fifth Avenue | 08-27-15 | ---- | 12-01-16 |
| 630 Park Avenue | 04-04-16 | ---- | 05-21-17 |
| 550 Park Avenue | 05-24-16 | ---- | 12-11-17 |
| 115 East 82nd Street | 04-08-19 | 06-10-19 | 05-21-21 |
| 4 East 66th Street (845 Fifth Avenue) | 04-30-19 | 07-24-19 | 1920 |
| 950 Park Avenue | 08-08-19 | 01-15-20 | 02-24-21 |
| 30 Central Park South | 08-19-19 | 03-21-20 | 05-20-21 |
| 145 East 52nd Street (demolished) | 11-24-19 | 09-23-20 | 05-03-21 |
| 920 Fifth Avenue | 09-06-21 | 11-09-21 | 10-11-22 |
| 1148 Fifth Avenue | 11-23-21 | 08-28-22 | 1923 |
| 1143 Fifth Avenue | 08-15-22 | 10-09-22 | 07-31-23 |
| 1060 Park Avenue | 08-26-22 | 02-13-23 | 02-29-24 |
| 4 East 95th Street | 12-04-22 | 03-15-23 | 02-27-24 |
| 580 Park Avenue | 12-12-22 | 02-27-23 | 10-29-23 |
| 620 Park Avenue | 05-08-23 | 12-15-23 | 07-10-24 |
| 655 Park Avenue | 07-31-23 | 10-16-23 | 09-03-24 |
| 1150 Fifth Avenue | 1923 | 1923 | 1924 |
| 145 East 73rd Street | 04-16-24 | 09-09-24 | 07-11-25 |
| 455 East 51st Street (consultant only) | 06-06-24 | 07-24-24 | 12-30-24 |
| 1030 Fifth Avenue | 06-30-24 | 09-15-24 | 10-15-25 |
| 1120 Fifth Avenue | 10-06-24 | 11-10-24 | 08-18-25 |
| 610 Park Avenue | 12-04-24 | 02-18-25 | 10-08-25 |
| 173–175 Riverside Drive | 07-07-25 | 09-21-25 | 02-09-27 |
| 1165 Fifth Avenue | 07-13-25 | 09-14-25 | 10-06-26 |
| 1170 Fifth Avenue | 1925 | 1925 | 1926 |
| 1035 Fifth Avenue | 07-25-25 | 10-28-25 | 10-25-26 |
| 1115 Fifth Avenue | 10-02-25 | 12-02-25 | 10-13-26 |
| 988 Fifth Avenue | 10-02-25 | 12-08-25 | 1926 |
| 810 Fifth Avenue | 10-02-25 | 12-17-25 | 1926 |
| 112 Central Park South | 10-02-25 | 11-24-26 | 10-25-27 |

| | | | |
|---|---|---|---|
| 170 East 79th Street | 01-07-26 | ---- | 10-15-26 |
| 950 Fifth Avenue | 04-13-26 | 05-13-26 | 01-05-27 |
| 825 Fifth Avenue | 08-10-26 | 12-10-26 | 10-05-27 |
| 812 Park Avenue | 01-11-27 | 02-08-27 | 10-04-27 |
| 1060 Fifth Avenue | 05-04-27 | 08-02-27 | 08-28-28 |
| 14 East 90th Street | 1928 | 1928 | 09-29 |
| 625 Park Avenue | 11-20-28 | 02-28-29 | 09-19-29 |
| 1 East 88th Street (1070 Fifth Avenue) (demolished) | ---- | | 1929 |
| 401 East 58th Street (studio apartments) 1929 | | | not built |
| 120 East 79th Street (13 stories) | 1929 | | not built |

# Chapter 3

## Rosario Candela

Rosario Candela (1890–1953) was born in Palermo, Sicily, and came to the United States at age nineteen to assist his father, a plasterer. Despite his shortage of funds, he managed to attend Columbia University School of Architecture and graduated in 1915. He apprenticed to Gaetano Ajello, an established apartment house architect and fellow Sicilian. After moving to the office of Frederick Sterner, an architect who specialized in townhouse modernizations, Candela established his own architectural office in 1920. Candela's first major commission came from Anthony Campagna and Joseph Paterno for the design of the Clayton apartment building at 215 W. Ninety-Second Street. This project produced the first of Candela's unique apartment house designs with a large entrance lobby and desirable floor layouts. Candela received a second Campagna commission for an elegant five-story walk-up on West 169th Street near Broadway.

During the next five years, Candela designed a number of residential buildings on the Upper West Side, primarily on West End Avenue and Riverside Drive. It was during this period that the West Side of Manhattan was undergoing an intense transformation from single-family homes to apartment buildings. Candela's return to the East Side in 1925 produced the elaborate and expensive 1

Sutton Place South with a grand porte cochere. The building featured expensive twelve- and thirteen-room simplex and duplex apartments along with a riverfront garden, indoor tennis court, and a private yacht landing pier directly on the East River.

In the same year, Candela designed two large buildings on Park Avenue, each including three- and four-bedroom apartments. He also designed the Stanhope Hotel at 985 Fifth Avenue opposite McKim, Mead, & White's 998 Fifth Avenue, which had been a pioneer high-rise apartment house. Candela produced eight more West Side buildings in 1925. He also designed the neo-Tudor six-story Fox Lane Apartments and Cambridge Court in Flushing, Queens for developer Edgar Ellinger.

By the late 1920s, Candela was the architect of choice for luxury apartments, employing fifty draftsmen. At a time when wealthy city dwellers were giving up their large private houses, Candela's apartments offered gracious dimensions, high ceilings, large windows, working fireplaces, maid's quarters, and opulent detailing.

The exteriors of his buildings tended to be understated while he was considered a master of design when it came to the interiors. Many of his apartments were constructed as duplex residences with grand entry foyers, curved and freestanding stairways, dramatic bedrooms and bathrooms, and spectacular public rooms. John D. Rockefeller Jr.'s triplex at 740 Park Avenue was palatial by the standards of the day. That triplex of twenty thousand square feet had from twenty-three to thirty-seven rooms, depending on whether you included hallways, foyers, servants' quarters, reception rooms, and the fourteen spacious bathrooms.

In 1927, Candela produced one of his greatest designs in 960 Fifth Avenue with an intricate three-dimensional network of interlocking apartments that included simplex units on one level and stacked duplex units and semi-duplex apartments on two levels that permitted extra-height ceilings in the reception rooms with more intimate proportions for the bedrooms. The structure also included a privately staffed kitchen and suite of dining rooms on the ground floor for the exclusive use of the building's tenants.

In 1928, Candela filed plans for nine buildings, including 720 Park Avenue that was completed the day before the 1929 stock market crash. Nevertheless, millionaire Jesse Isador Strauss maintained the huge terraced duplex, which his widow occupied it until her death in 1970.

Candela's six grandest apartment houses were filed from March to October 1929: 740 Park Avenue, 770 Park Avenue, 778 Park Avenue, 1220 Park Avenue, 834 Fifth Avenue, and 1040 Fifth Avenue. These apartments are rated by experts as the most magnificent collection by any architect. They were built and completed just before the Great Depression took effect.

Despite the sharp reduction in Candela's workload, from twenty-six commissions in 1929 to two in 1930 and one in 1931, Candela's commissions increased in 1936, 1937, 1939, and 1940. By then, World War II stopped all nonessential construction. However, during the 1930s, Candela joined with the theater designer Thomas Lamb to produce the Rialto Theater Building, which included a 750-seat movie theater, stores, offices, and a restaurant on the top floor.

During the Depression, Candela served as a visiting design critic for New York's Beaux Arts Institute of Design and wrote,

> An apartment, excepting a one-room unit, is composed of two well defined sections depending

on which of the 24 hours of one's daily life it is used; the living quarters and the sleeping quarters, and in the case of luxurious apartments, a third one, the service quarters. An ideal apartment, regardless of its size, must have these two or three sections segregated, not infringing on each other, and easily connected to one another, with the living section nearest to the entrance.

Candela began studying cryptography in the 1930s after reading *The American Black Chamber* by Herbert Yardley. Candela taught a course on cryptography starting in 1941 and wrote two books on the subject: *Isomorphism and Its Application in Cryptoanalytics* and *The Military Cipher of Commandment Bazeries*. Starting in 1941, Candela taught a course on cryptography and cryptanalytics at Hunter College in New York. At the time, the course was considered the only one of its kind offered to the public in the United States. When World War II started, he worked for the OSS, which was the forerunner of the CIA. At his death on October 6, 1953, at age sixty-three, he was writing a third book on the subject.

Virtually all of Candela's seventy-five apartment buildings are still standing, many protected by the New York Landmark Preservation Law.

On May 17, 2018, the first exhibition, "Elegance in the Sky: The Architecture of Rosario Candela," opened at the Museum of the City of New York.

# Chronology of Candela New York Apartment Houses

| Address | Filed | Begun | Completed |
|---|---|---|---|
| 215 West 92nd Street | 01–09–22 | 01–31–22 | 10–05–22 |
| 559 West 169th Street | 02–21–22 | 03–16–22 | 07–19–22 |
| 915 West End Avenue | 04–10–22 | 08–28–22 | 03–24–23 |
| 881 St. Nicholas Avenue | 04–25–22 | 04–29–22 | 09–22–22 |
| 878 West End Avenue | 05–24–22 | 10–26–22 | 05–18–23 |
| 304 West 89th Street | 06–10–22 | 09–18–22 | 05–16–23 |
| 1105 Park Avenue | 10–26–22 | 03–12–23 | 10–30–23 |
| 680 Riverside Drive | 12–26–22 | 01–18–23 | 08–23–23 |
| 29 Spring Street | 03–28–23 | 09–06–23 | 07–07–24 |
| 300 West 108th Street | 09–08–23 | 11–12–23 | 07–09–24 |
| 875 West End Avenue | 11–07–23 | 01–18–24 | 10–07–24 |
| 522 West End Avenue | 11–23–23 | 01–19–24 | 09–20–24 |
| 41 Fifth Avenue | 12–04–23 | ---- | 10–10–24 |
| 332 West 86th Street | 12–14–23 | 02–26–24 | 09–18–24 |
| 240 West End Avenue | 12–19–23 | 02–26–24 | 09–24–24 |
| 519 West 139th Street | 03–04–24 | 04–08–24 | 08–28–24 |
| 40 West 55th Street | 03–08–24 | 06–24–24 | 01–13–25 |
| 1 Adrian Avenue, The Bronx | 03–26–24 | ---- | 09–25–24 |
| 425 Riverside Drive | 05–16–24 | 06–23–24 | 1925 |
| 755 West End Avenue | 07–25–24 | 12–04–24 | 09–15–25 |
| 161 W 75th and 174 W 76th Streets | 10–06–24 | 12–15–24 | 11–05–25 |
| 1 Sutton Place South | 01–28–25 | ---- | 01–27–26 |
| 800 West End Avenue | 04–25–25 | 07–10–25 | 01–22–26 |
| 315 West 106th Street | 07–28–25 | 02–04–26 | 07–29–26 |
| 1172 Park Avenue | 1925 | 1925 | 1926 |
| 280 Riverside Drive | 08–07–25 | 10–09–25 | 07–06–26 |
| 1192 Park Avenue | 08–19–25 | 01–29–26 | 10–08–26 |
| 285 Riverside Drive | 08–20–25 | 10–09–25 | 06–01–26 |
| 325 West 86th Street | 08–29–25 | 11–05–25 | 06–25–26 |
| 607 West End Avenue | 09–03–25 | 10–19–25 | 04–30–26 |
| Fox Lane Apts (38th Ave and Bowne St, Flushing, Queens) 1925 1926 | | | |
| 995 Fifth Avenue | 10–21–25 | ---- | 09–20–26 |
| 120 East 56th Street | 10–28–25 | 01–21–26 | 10–19–26 |
| 820 West End Avenue | 11–21–25 | 01–27–26 | 07–29–26 |
| 100 West 58th Street | 01–18–26 | ---- | 10–28–26 |
| 39 Plaza Street, Brooklyn | ---- | ---- | 1926 |

| | | | |
|---|---|---|---|
| 150 West 58th Street | 02–17–26 | 05–17–26 | 03–14–27 |
| 130 East 39th Street | 04–27–26 | 09–18–26 | 05–16–27 |
| 990 Fifth Avenue | 08–30–26 | 11–04–26 | 10–14–27 |
| 775 Park Avenue | 09–16–26 | 11–15–26 | 10–18–27 |
| 230 West End Avenue | 02–16–27 | 03–01–27 | 10–07–27 |
| 2 East 70th Street | 03–09–27 | 04–16–27 | 02–18–28 |
| Cambridge Court (37th Ave and Bowne St, Flushing, Queens) ---- | | | 05–28 |
| 856 Fifth Avenue (2 East Sixty-Seventh Street) | 08–03–27 | 10–10–27 | 10–04–28 |
| 960 Fifth Avenue | 08–22–27 | 09–20–27 | 11–28–28 |
| 447 East 57th Street | 10–09–27 | 12–07–27 | 10–04–28 |
| 25 Sutton Place | 11–01–27 | 12–25–27 | 08–02–28 |
| 307 West 57th Street | 11–14–27 | 12–08–27 | 10–11–28 |
| 47 Plaza Street, Brooklyn | 12–27 | ---- | Fall 28 |
| 30 Sutton Place | 11–28–27 | 01–11–28 | 08–29–28 |
| 8 East 96th Street | 12–15–27 | 12–22–27 | 10–06–28 |
| 19 East 98th Street | 01–11–28 | 02–16–28 | 10–02–28 |
| 70 East 96th Street | 02–15–28 | 11–20–28 | 07–15–29 |
| 720 Park Avenue | 02–21–28 | ---- | 09–28–29 |
| 40 West Sixty-Seventh Street | 06–26–28 | 08–31–28 | 06–06–29 |
| 360 Central Park West | 08–09–28 | 10–30–28 | 10–04–29 |
| 175 West 93rd Street | 08–25–28 | 11–23–28 | 07–23–29 |
| 75 Central Park West | 10–19–28 | 01–26–29 | 09–25–29 |
| 1 Gracie Square | 12–18–28 | 01–16–29 | 08–19–29 |
| 40 East 66th Street | 12–18–28 | 01–22–29 | 08–30–29 |
| 4 Sutton Place | 01–03–29 | ---- | 04–17–30 |
| 1025 Park Avenue | 01–05–29 | 03–12–29 | 09–26–29 |
| 14 Sutton Place South | 01–09–29 | 02–04–29 | 11–27–29 |
| 127 West 57th Street (attributed to Candela) | 02–11–29 | 09–26–29 | 07–30–29 |
| 770 Park Avenue | 03–11–29 | 10–14–29 | 09–15–30 |
| 778 Park Avenue | 03–13–29 | 08–29–29 | 07–08–31 |
| 740 Park Avenue | 03–13–29 | 11–11–29 | 09–16–30 |
| 1220 Park Avenue | 09–10–29 | 09–23–29 | 10–03–30 |
| 834 Fifth Avenue | 09–18–29 | 10–21–29 | 05–09–31 |
| 1040 Fifth Avenue | 09–24–29 | 01–04–30 | 10–08–30 |
| 340 East 57th Street | 10–03–29 | 12–05–29 | 09–25–30 |
| 133 East 80th Street | 10–30–29 | 01–04–30 | 08–19–30 |
| 450 East 58th Street (14 stories, 14 units) | | 1929 | not built |
| 225 East 69th Street | | 1929 | not built |
| 1 East 79th Street | | 1929 | not built |

| | | | |
|---|---|---|---|
| 333 East 79th Street | | 1929 | not built |
| 160 West 80th Street (16 stories, 160 units) | | 1929 | not built |
| 537 East Eighty-Second Street | | 1929 | not built |
| 510 East 86th Street (15 stories, 62 units) | | 1929 | not built |
| 120 East 89th Street (12 stories, 109 units) | | 1929 | not built |
| 1074 Fifth Avenue (14 stories, 14 units) | | 1929 | not built |
| 750 Park Avenue (18 stories, 35 units) | | 1929 | not built |
| 799 Park Avenue (18 stories, 25 units) | | 1929 | not built |
| 1245 Park Avenue | | 1929 | not built |
| 222 Riverside Drive (15 stories, 109 units) | | 1929 | not built |
| 225 West End Ave (15 stories, 153 units) | | 1929 | not built |
| Watergate Apts (East River and 48th and 49th Streets) | | 1929 | not built |
| 12 East 88th Street | 11–08–30 | 12–19–30 | 06–04–31 |
| 56 Seventh Avenue | 11–19–30 | 03–17–31 | 11–19–31 |
| 2 Beekman Place | 01–08–31 | 02–26–31 | 12–16–32 |
| 530 Park Avenue | | | 1934 not built |
| 19 East 72nd Street | 09–29–36 | ---- | 09–25–37 |
| 955 Fifth Avenue | 10–22–37 | 01–06–38 | 07–21–38 |
| 248 East 46th Street | 1939 | 05–16–39 | 10–26–39 |
| 44 East Sixty-Seventh Street | 07–03–40 | 09–06–40 | 06–20–41 |
| 1 East 66th Street (850 Fifth Avenue) (with Paul Resnick) | 01–28–48 | 07–28–48 | 11–17–50 |
| 135 East 54th Street (with Paul Resnick) | 12–02–48 | 10–26–49 | 12–05–50 |

# Chapter 4

## Harrison Albright

Harrison Albright (1866–1932) was born in the Philadelphia area and began his career there, but he successfully transferred his practice to Charleston, West Virginia, and Los Angeles, California, and achieved more fame than for his early work in Philadelphia. Albright was born in Shoemakertown (now Ogontz), Pennsylvania, the son of Joseph and Louise Adele (Jeannot) Albright. He was educated in the public schools, Pierce College of Business, and Spring Garden Institute in Philadelphia, where he won second prize in the drawings competition of 1883. Albright spent six years in apprenticeship: four years with George T. Pearson and two with Cabot, Chandler, and Boyden.

By April 1886, Albright had established an independent office at 508 Walnut Street where his career flourished, with many residences in the Oak Lane area of the city as well as the police, fire, and patrol houses. By 1887, Albright's practice extended into New Jersey and to Buffalo, New York, so that he could oversee the pavilion and boat landing, which he had designed for a site near Wilson Harbor on Lake Ontario.

Unfortunately, in December 1890, the *Philadelphia Real Estate Record and Builders Guide* reported that Albright had been exonerated in a trial for conspiracy to defraud a client, one E. N. Manning of Elm Station. Perhaps this adverse publicity persuaded Albright that it was time to move on from Philadelphia, and by 1891, he had established an office in Charleston, West Virginia, where he remained until 1905, when he moved to Los Angeles. Albright's designs in West Virginia included civic, institutional, residential, and collegiate work, but for the last several years of his career in West Virginia, he concentrated on the design and construction of fireproof hotels, including the Richmond Hotel in Richmond, Virginia, and the West Baden Springs Hotel in West Baden, Indiana.

In 1855, the Mile Lick Inn was built to capitalize on the abundance of mineral springs in the area. The name was later changed to West Baden Springs Hotel since it was fashioned after Baden-Baden, the great mineral spa of Europe. Lee W. Sinclair transformed West Baden into a sophisticated resort, adding an opera house, a casino, a two-deck pony and bicycle track, and a full-sized baseball field. Sadly, in June of 1901 a fire destroyed the entire lodging structure in less than two hours. Thankfully, all of the guests escaped harm.

Sinclair used this tragedy as his opportunity to build the hotel of his dreams. He envisioned a circular building topped with the world's largest dome, decorated like the grandest spas of Europe. Architect Harrison Albright of West Virginia accepted Sinclair's commission and agreed to complete the project within a year. The new hotel, complete with a two hundred-foot-diameter atrium and fireplace that burned fourteen-foot logs, opened for business in June 1902.

After Sinclair died in 1916, his daughter, Lillian, and her husband took over the hotel's operation and completed a massive renovation effort that left their finances overextended. In 1923, Lillian sold the hotel to Ed Ballard for $1 million.

When the stock market crashed in 1929, the hotel emptied of guests almost overnight. Ballard eventually closed the hotel in June 1932, and in 1934, he sold it to the Jesuits for one dollar. The Jesuits removed many of property's elegant appointments and eventually dismantled the building's four Moorish towers. The seminary, known as West Baden College, operated until 1964 when declining enrollment led the Jesuits to close the facility. A Michigan couple purchased the property in 1966 and donated it to Northwood Institute, a private college that operated in the building until 1983.

While the colleges did not maintain the West Baden property in the same lavish style of the hotel in its prime, it was relatively well cared for until 1985 when Northwood sold it to a real estate development firm. That firm soon declared bankruptcy, and the property was tangled in years of litigation.

In 1974, West Baden was listed as a National Historic Landmark, but the elements took their toll on the neglected hotel, and it was closed to the public in 1989 for safety reasons. In January 1991, a buildup of ice and water on the roof and in drainpipes caused the collapse of a portion of the exterior wall. Indiana Landmarks, the country's largest statewide historic preservation organization, led the charge to stabilize the hotel to preserve redevelopment potential, and attract a new owner capable of restoring the property. In 1992, Indiana Landmarks spent $140,000 to stabilize the hotel, matching a $70,000 contribution from an anonymous donor.

In May 1994, the hotel was sold to Minnesota Investment Partners for $500,000. Grand Casinos Inc., an investor in the purchase, optioned the hotel from MIP and with the Cook Group Inc., a global medical device manufacturing company headquartered nearby in Bloomington, stepped in to preserve both the French Lick and West Baden Springs Hotels. Under the direction of Bill and Gayle Cook and their son Carl, both hotels and their grounds received a multimillion-dollar renovation, returning them to the grandeur of the days of Sinclair and uniting them as one resort. In 2006, French Lick Springs Hotel reopened after an extensive renovation and a new addition, the French Lick Casino. The original 1917 "Hill Course" was reopened and restored as the Donald Ross Golf Course. With the completion of the West Baden Springs Hotel restoration in 2007, the French Lick Resort was born.

The West Baden Springs Hotel was named a National Historic Landmark in 1987. In 2008, *Condé Nast* magazine ranked the hotel twenty-first on its list of the "Top 75 Mainland US Resorts." In 2009, the American Automobile Association recognized the hotel as one of the top ten historic hotels in the United States and awarded it a four-diamond rating. A Zagat Survey in 2009 included the hotel on its list of "Top US Hotels, Resorts, and Spas."

The National Trust for Historic Preservation has included the hotel in its Historic Hotels of America program. The American Society of Civil Engineers designated the hotel as a National Historic Civil Engineering Landmark.

Harrison Albright's office in Los Angeles opened on March 28, 1905, and his career in California, where he resided until his death, built upon his experience with fireproof hotels, most notably the U. S. Grant Hotel in San Diego, and included work for the Santa Fe Railroad. He experimented with reinforced concrete and held the distinction of employing John Lloyd Wright, son of Frank Lloyd Wright, in his firm at the time of the design of the Golden West Hotel at 720 South Fourth Street in San Diego.

In short order, Albright obtained a commission for an annex to the Laughlin Building. Homer Laughlin (1843–1913) won a municipal competition to build a ceramics factory in East Liverpool, Ohio, in 1872, a town directly across the Ohio River. Opened in 1874, Laughlin's business became phenomenally successful, requiring the factory to expand several times before Laughlin sold his interest in it in 1897 and moved to California. According to the architectural biographer, Henry Whitney, Albright's main work in the city was the ten-story Consolidated Realty Building, on the southwest corner of Hill Street and Sixth Street, built in 1907. He worked as an architect for the Santa Fe Railroad and designed the predecessor to Union Station in Los Angeles (now demolished) and the terminal at Ash Forks, Arizona. He designed a number of notable buildings in San Diego, including the U. S. Grant Hotel and the San Diego Public Library.

The U. S. Grant Hotel was built by U. S. Grant Jr. in honor of his illustrious father, President Ulysses S. Grant. Grant bought the hundred-room Horton House Hotel and demolished it to construct the current hotel in 1910.

In 1906, San Francisco was devastated by a massive earthquake that was felt as far south as San Diego. Upon rebuilding San Francisco, the original lobby plans for the U. S. Grant were provided to the developers of the Palace Hotel in San Francisco who created the Garden Court that was originally intended for the U. S. Grant Hotel. When it opened, the U. S. Grant Hotel featured top floor arcadia windows, balcony balustrades, and imposing lentil cornices. Inside, a grand white marble staircase with a carved alabaster railing led from the lobby up to the hotel rooms. In 1919, Baron Long acquired an interest in the hotel and for the next twenty years instituted the following improvements:

- converted the hotel's Bivouac Grill into a profitable speakeasy during Prohibition, the Plata Real nightclub, with live music and dancing and illegal beverages
- created the Italianate Ballroom on the lower level with a travertine marble floor and a unique hand-painted ceiling (now the Crystal Ballroom)
- installed the tallest radio towers on the West Coast on the hotel's roof, which became the home offices for radio station KFVW. President Franklin Roosevelt delivered one of his first radio speeches to the country from this radio station.

When the U. S. Grant Hotel went through another ownership change after World War II, the second-floor Palm Court was enclosed to create the Palm Pavilion, and the Grand Ballroom on the ninth floor was converted to guest rooms. But perhaps the most successful decision was to create the Grant Grill off the lobby on Fourth Avenue. After sit-ins by a group of female attorneys in 1969, the Grant Grill ended its "men's-only" policy. As a tribute to these brave women, a brass plaque was installed outside the Grant Grill to commemorate the end of that discriminatory policy.

The hotel was extensively refurnished in the early 1980s by the New York-based Sybedon Corporation and Christopher Kit Sickels.

Disclosure: I served as the hotel consultant to the Sybedon Corporation who succeeded in coming up with the funds for a spectacular renovation and reopening of the U. S. Grant Hotel in December 1985.

At about the same time that the hotel renovation project was underway, a twenty-six-square-block, uniquely designed shopping mall, the Horton Plaza, opened across the street from the Grant Hotel. It was designed by the well-known architect John Jerde, and it attracted twenty-five million people in its first year. The area was further invigorated by the massive restoration of the Gaslamp Quarter and the relocation of the San Diego Convention Center to Harbor Drive.

In 2003, the hotel was purchased by the very ancestors of the land on which it stood. Sycuan Tribal Development Corporation (STDC), the business arm of the sovereign tribe of the Kumeyaay Nation, acquired the eleven-story hotel for $45 million.

The Kumeyaay Indians are one of four Native American tribes that are indigenous to San Diego County. The Kumeyaay can trace their San Diego roots back more than ten thousand years. Their people lived on the northern edges of San Diego and south past the Mexican border, with land that includes the very spot where the U. S. Grant now stands.

President Ulysses S. Grant, the eighteenth president of the United States, disapproved of the treatment of the Indians of the American West. In 1875, he passed an executive order setting aside 640 acres of land in Dehasa Valley in East San Diego County for the Kumeyaay Tribes. In great part due to his efforts, the United States government in 1891 passed the "Act for the Relief of the Mission Indians," which officially recognized the sovereign status of California's Indian tribes.

The Kumeyaay, who had suffered enormously at the hands of generations of white westerners, remember Ulysses S. Grant as a rare soul among politicians—forthright and generous. He gave them what so many before attempted to take away: dignity in the form of land. In an act of poetic and economic justice, the extraordinary restoration of the U. S. Grant Hotel pays respect to its history and to the heritage of the Kumeyaay Nation.

In 2006, the U. S. Grant Hotel reopened in time for its ninety-sixth anniversary after a twenty-one-month, $56 million restoration. During the renovation, unexpected surprises kept turning up original treasures. After removing the carpet on the grand staircase, workers realized the original white Italian marble was still intact although damaged. The staircase posts and balustrades, thought to be made of wood, turned out to be carved alabaster. To complement these unexpected treasures, rare white marble with gray vein was installed at the base of the staircase and throughout the lobby. After this extraordinary restoration, the U. S. Grant became a member of Starwood's Luxury Collection.

From the time of the opening of the Horton House Hotel until today, the U. S. Grant has hosted many celebrities, including fourteen US presidents from Woodrow Wilson to John F. Kennedy to George W. Bush—and the world-famous aviator Charles Lindbergh. More recently, celebrities like Bruce Willis, Demi Moore, and Governor Arnold Schwarzenegger have stayed at the U. S. Grant Hotel.

Harrison Albright became a favorite designer of John D. Spreckels (1853–1926), a California real estate and transportation magnate (John D. Spreckels was heir to the huge fortune in sugar amassed by his father, Claus Spreckels). For John D. Spreckels (1853–1926), Albright designed five buildings in California, including the Spreckels House (Coronado Beach, 1908), the Spreckels Theater (San Diego, 1912), and the Spreckels Organ Pavilion, (Balboa Park,

San Diego, 1915). For this client and others, Albright established himself as a notable proponent of reinforced concrete construction in Southern California; he retired for health reasons in 1925 and died at his home in Los Angeles eight years later.

# Chapter 5

## Hiss & Weekes

### Philip Hiss (1857–1940) and H. Hobart Weekes (1867–1950)

Philip Hiss was born in 1857 in Baltimore, Maryland. He was educated in the public schools of Baltimore and began architectural studies under private tutors.

H. Hobart Weekes as born in 1867 in New York and attended Trinity Church School. From 1883 to 1886, he studied architecture and sculpture in the United States, England, France, Italy, and Greece. He was a draftsman and designer for the well-known firm of McKim, Mead, & White from 1886 until 1899 when he established a partnership with architect Philip Hiss, which lasted until 1933.

Hiss & Weekes designed churches, banks, apartment houses, and large private residences in both city and country settings. Among its most famous projects were the Gotham Hotel and the Belnord Apartments in New York and the Elizabeth Arden Building in Chicago.

# Gotham/Peninsula Hotel New York

The original Gotham Hotel is one of the few structures on Fifth Avenue that recalls the golden age of luxury hotels and the prominent place they occupied in the formation of the city. Erected in 1905, it was designed by the architectural firm of Hiss & Weekes and is among the oldest of the early "skyscraper" hotels. These hotels heralded the transformation of Fifth Avenue from an exclusive residential street—Millionaires' Row—to a fashionable commercial thoroughfare. Rising twenty stories, including a multistoried rooftop addition, at the southwest corner of West Fifty-Fifth Street and Fifth Avenue, the boldly rendered Gotham was a stylistic counterpoint to its contemporary, the flamboyant Beaux-Arts St. Regis Hotel, which was directly across Fifth Avenue. It also skillfully complemented McKim, Mead, & White's University Club, which adjoins the Peninsula to the south.

The *Architectural Record* reported in November 1902:

> We all know how woefully individualistic our builders have been, resulting in a mass of fragmentary, inharmonious, clashing architecture, no attempt being made to work in common for the sake of beauty and uniformity. This great projected hotel (the Gotham) of eighteen stories is designed to harmonize with the adjacent University Club, which is a fine piece of architecture. The architectural lines of the hotel will follow the lines of the University Club. The same centre line will make a continuous arcade of five openings in the club and five in the hotel. The stone balustrade will be carried out on the same lines of the present balustrade of the club.

Thus the whole block will be tied together. The general scheme of architecture is also the same as that of the club, being Italian Renaissance as far as possible in an eighteen storied building.

The firm of Hiss & Weekes continued in practice for thirty-four years, producing a number of buildings in the city, including the spectacular Belnord Apartments (1908–09), a massive neo-Italian Renaissance apartment house on West Eighty-Sixth Street (a designated New York City Landmark), and the handsome Beaux-Arts townhouses at 6 and 8 West Sixty-Fifth Street (now in the Upper East Side Historic District).

The Gotham Hotel never seemed to find the favor it sought, in part because it was overshadowed by the subsequent openings of the opulent St. Regis Hotel across Fifth Avenue and then the Plaza Hotel four blocks to the north. The Gotham was foreclosed in 1908 after it failed to get a liquor license. As Christopher Gray reported in his Streetscapes article in the *New York Times* (January 3, 1999):

> The Fifth Avenue Presbyterian Church is at the northwest corner of 55th and Fifth and the St. Regis had just barely won permission to serve liquor—it was in technical violation of a restriction prohibiting liquor sales within 200 feet of a church. The Gotham, directly across 55th Street from the church was unequivocally in violation of the law. Several newspaper accounts state that United States Senator Thomas C. Platt and other influential politicians were silent partners on the original Gotham team, and in 1905 and 1907 bills were introduced in the

New York State Legislature exempting hotels from the provision if they had more than 200 rooms.

Neither of the bills, which were clearly fashioned for the Gotham, passed. In 1908 the Gotham went into foreclosure over a $741 butcher's bill, and the *Real Estate Record and Guide* said that the failure was due solely to the liquor restriction, which it denounced as ludicrous. The hotel, which had cost $4 million to build, was sold for $2.45 million.

The hotel was sold in 1920 to William & Julius Manger, proprietors of the Manger chain of hotels, including the Martha Washington Hotel for Women. Subsequently, the Kirkeby Hotel Group purchased the property in 1944. Other owners were Mrs. Evelyn Sharp, Webb & Knapp, Wellington Associates, Swiss hotel owner Rene Hatt, Sol Goldman, Irving Goldman, Arthur Cohen, William Zeckendorf Jr., and Steven Goodstein. Finally, in 1988, the Hong Kong and Shanghai Hotels Ltd., the parent company of the Peninsula Group of hotels in Asia, bought the Gotham Hotel for $127 million and renamed it the Peninsula Hotel. At last, the Gotham got the owner it had needed since 1905. If you ever stayed at the original Peninsula Hotel in Hong Kong, you know what true luxury and service really feel like: complimentary fruit and champagne in your room while watching the Star Ferry cross the harbor outside your window; a Rolls-Royce for guest transportation to meetings and the airport; savoring a double espresso in the busy lobby bar while reading the *International Herald Tribune.*

The New York Peninsula Hotel has received the AAA Five Diamond Award for thirteen consecutive years. The Peninsula has one of the best and biggest hotel health clubs in New York, including a thirty-five thousand-square-foot spa, a glass-enclosed swimming pool, and the rooftop bar and terrace.

The hotel has opted for an amenity that is more sporty than chic: chauffeur-driven Mini Coopers. The cars are available for up to three hours a day to guests who book a suite. Passengers can follow city tours that are stored on iPhones or iPads in the cars—or they can simply tell drivers where they want to go. The cars, the Mini Cooper S Clubman model, have been customized to hold a mini-refrigerator and a cargo box on top for shopping bags. Aside from the make, the main difference between these and the Hong Kong fleet is that you won't get a trip to the airport. These vehicles are intended strictly for local joyrides.

On February 7, 1989, the Peninsula Hotel was designated as a landmark by the New York Landmarks Preservation Commission. The old Gotham is an orphan no more.

## Belnord Apartments New York

The Belnord is one of a handful of full-block apartment buildings that are built around a large, landscaped interior courtyard. The Belnord's courtyard is one of the largest in the city. It is a New York City landmark, which was added to the National Register of Historic Places in 1980. The famous architect Robert A. M. Stern is in the process of renovating the once-segmented apartments as they become available to provide maximum light and living space. Stern describes the Belnord as follows:

> It belongs to this special sequence of New York building: courtyard apartments, grand palazzi,

which began with the Dakota in 1880, designed by Henry Hardenbergh. Other notables in the genre include Charles Platt's Astor Place, Clinton and Russell's Graham Court and The Apthorp, and 1185 Park Avenue by Schwartz & Gross. Many more fell victim to New York's various building booms and have since been razed to make way for high-rise office towers.

Situated between Eighty-Sixth and Eighty-Seventh Streets and Broadway and Amsterdam Avenues, the Belnord has seen Manhattan grow around it. When Stern was asked how the neighborhood affected his design process, he replied, "Maybe we should ask the question the other way around. The building has been here almost before the neighborhood." With Astor Court, the Apthorp, and William Earle Dodge Stokes and Paul E. Duboy's the Ansonia (once called "the grandest hotel in Manhattan") in close proximity, "the Belnord sits in very good apartment-house company," Stern says. And no surprise:

> It had an incredible location. The subway only opened two years before the building was created-right at Eighty-Sixth Street. But also it's midway between Central Park and Riverside Park, so all you have to do when you come out the front door is make up your mind which park you're going to go to that day. Then, since Eighty-Sixth Street is a wide street, it has a lot of trees, and of course it's been narrowed since then like all sidewalks have, but you still get the feeling of a nice, landscaped street."

The Belnord, Stern says, "adds class to the neighborhood-an immeasurable amount of class!" Of course, it's also a product of its past; the building's history, Stern found when he first visited, is quite literally ingrained in it—and not always in the most aesthetically pleasing manner. "Over the decades, the apartments have been renovated and opened up in different ways, often quite clumsily done," the architect says. "Our job is to restore dignity to the plans, following the kind of organizational principles of clear, defined rooms that I think Weekes had in mind in 1908, and having our rooms unfold logically in a nice sequence."

To do so, Stern and his team will open up once-segmented apartments, which are being renovated as they're vacated, to afford for maximum light and living space and follow an intuitive layout. "The original apartments were interestingly laid out from a geometric point of view," Stern explains. "They were rather small by modern standards. For example, what they labeled on the original plans as a parlor and we would, I suppose, call a living room, were in some cases smaller than the bedrooms." Keeping in mind today's preference for fewer walls, Stern will expand the living spaces and join them with the dining rooms and kitchens, newly transformed from cramped staff quarters to open-plan versions, "which make them much more spacious-feeling and really much more appropriate for the twenty-first century," the architect says.

For the bedrooms, Stern will stick more closely to the original layout. "The building has an amazing courtyard, which not only provides a private oasis for the residents but also made it possible to lay out apartments that are either corner apartments or floor-through apartments," he notes. "So typically—and we are following this procedure—the bedrooms are on the courtside, which is quieter, and the living rooms and kitchens are on the street side."

In the building's public spaces, which will get a double dose of design star power with Rafael de Cárdenas at work on their amenities suite, preservation reigned supreme. "We tried to save a lot of the materials, particularly on the interior floor vestibules, where there's beautiful mosaic tiles that are almost completely intact," Stern says.

Where new materials were needed, Stern stuck to a classic palette inspired, in part, by Dorothy Draper's original design for the Carlyle: "We use a black-and-white vocabulary in the public spaces of the building-it speaks to 1908, but even more so I think it works well for 2018 and going forward." Aforementioned mosaics will be juxtaposed with Nero marble with black-and-white veining, hallway walls will be high-gloss white, and apartment doors will be a complementary black.

This palette carries over into the apartments: Kitchens will have counters and backsplashes of Calcutta gold, with a choice of white lacquer or cerused oak cabinetry. The master bath is swathed in Siberian white marble, while the guest bathrooms will have the same black-and-white marble as the lobby vestibules, Stern explains, "so there's a nice carry-through." We work from the same principles no matter what we do," says the architect. "We try to respect the past and be inventive with what we learn from the past. Often in a building, we look to the past and then interpret it to move forward. Here, we are looking to the past and encountering it directly."

As for the more extreme changes he made, Stern hopes they tie back better to the original plan than the renovations before them. "I hope

Mr. Weekes will forgive us for changing things; when we first walked in, my god, those apartments were not 1908, they were 1962," he says, laughing. "In reality, very little of his planning remains and what went on after him is—well, I'm doing a mercy killing."

All in the very worthy name, though, of preservation—not only of the past but for the future. "We have to design with the past in mind and to meet the requirements of the foreseeable future," Stern says. "I hope by the time there are enough of our apartments there—say, 2022 or '24, they will really bear the new, fresh Belnord."

# Chapter 6

## Schwartz & Gross

Schwartz & Gross was a New York City-based architectural firm that was active from 1901 until 1963. Along with the architects J. E. R. Carpenter and Rosario Candela, they probably designed more than 50 percent of the apartment hotels that were built in New York in the early twentieth century.

Simon I. Schwartz (1877–1956) and Arthur Gross (1877–1950) met as students at the Hebrew Technical Institute in the 1890s in Manhattan's East Village neighborhood. After working for other architectural firms, they founded their own company in 1902. They specialized in designing apartment hotels on the Upper East Side and West Side. Their firm was very successful and designed eight of the historic buildings on Central Park West that are designated as contributing properties of the Central Park West Historic District, including 55 Central Park West, known as the "Ghostbusters Building" after its prominent appearance in that 1984 movie.

One of their infamous buildings, the Majestic at 215 West Seventy-Fifth Street, was completed in 1924 as a brothel and de facto men's clubhouse with hidden stairways and secret doorways. Its clandestine activity attracted one of the most notorious tenants,

Polly Adler, who ran popular brothels in the 1920s in a succession of rented apartments. The full-fledged madam set up shop at the Majestic where prostitutes were the main but not the only attraction. Polly's was a clubhouse as well as a brothel. She designed her establishments in luxurious décor with Persian carpets, imported furniture, and original paintings. Members of the famous Algonquin Round Table were frequent guests, including *Vanity Fair* writers like Robert Benchley and Dorothy Parker (who wanted to experience the ambience of the place). Other patrons included the famous New York mayor Jimmy Walker as well as mob boss Dutch Schultz. Adler's all-night parties continued through Prohibition and featured illegal booze, backgammon, and card games as well as prostitution.

The Hotel Lincoln, at twenty-seven stories and 1,331 rooms, was the largest hotel in New York City when it opened on February 13, 1928, to the design of Schwartz & Gross. It featured a towering sign on the roof with neon lettering reading "Hotel Lincoln," which was lit on opening day when Governor Al Smith pressed a button in Albany to illuminate it. The sign is visible in the 1933 film *42nd Street*. The Hotel Lincoln was purchased by the prominent real estate developer William Zeckendorf in September 1957, and after extensive renovations, it was renamed the Manhattan Hotel. The existing Hotel Lincoln sign was removed in 1958 and replaced with an enormous letter "M," thirty-one feet wide by twelve feet deep. Zeckendorf sold the Manhattan Hotel to English investors who renamed it the Royal Manhattan Hotel. Famous entertainers like jazz pianist and bandleader Count Basie, saxophonist Lester Young, trumpeter Harry "Sweets" Edison, and clarinetist Artie Shaw performed in the Blue Room nightclub of the hotel.

In 1978, the Milstein family bought the hotel, renovated it, and reopened it in 1980 as the Milford Plaza Hotel. This enabled them to keep the huge "M" sign on the roof. For many years, the Milford Plaza used the song "Lullaby of Broadway" in their television advertisements.

In 2010, the Rockpoint Group and Highgate Holdings purchased the hotel for $200 million and began an extensive $140 million renovation, which included removal of the neon "M" sign atop of the building.

In February 2013, it was announced that the new owners would divide the hotel into three parts: a 1,331-room hotel, a 26,000-square-foot retail unit, and vacant land, which would sell for a combined value of $650 million. Soon thereafter, the Brooklyn-based investor David Werner, in partnership with Deutsche Asset and Wealth Management's real estate investment company, purchased the project for $325 million.

As part of the acquisition, the hotel was briefly renamed the Milford New York Hotel before being named in 2014 as Row NYC. An extensive renovation project refurnished all 1,331 guest rooms and suites, public and meeting spaces, the International Gift Shop and District M—a European express café by day and a Neapolitan pizza bar and cocktail lounge by night. A unique three-story, glass-enclosed lobby design and illuminated grand staircase was added with see-through guest elevators.

In his book *Morningside Heights: A History of Its Architecture and Development*, Andrew S. Dolkart wrote:

> The builders responsible for the development of most
> early twentieth-century apartment houses in New

York City and almost all of the apartment buildings
on Morningside Heights reflect the major changes
that were occurring in the city's ethnic composition
during this period, especially the immigration of
hundreds of thousands of Italians and Eastern
European Jews. The entry of immigrant Italians
and Jews and the children of these immigrants into
the worlds of real estate, building, and investment
coincided with the advent of the apartment building
as the most popular form of middle-class residence
in Manhattan. Speculative construction, sale, and
leasing of such buildings was not tied to social
connections, as was the construction of private
homes for the wealthy. In the nineteenth century,
a substantial proportion of the city's speculative
rowhouses had been erected by Irish builders,
while German immigrants had erected many of the
tenements on the Lower East Side. All one needed
to become involved in speculative development
was sufficient capital for the initial investment
in land and construction, and the ability to get a
loan. Many immigrants speculated in a small way,
often risking money on only one or two projects.
Others became professional builders, investing in
the construction of many buildings.

In 1898, John Paterno began construction on two
of the earliest apartment houses on Morningside
Heights, a pair of modest structures at 505 and
507 West 112th Street (demolished). At John's
death in 1899, Joseph and his brother Charles were
brought in to complete the unfinished buildings.

From this beginning, the Paterno brothers went on to contribute significantly to the construction of apartment houses in New York City, undertaking their "most extensive construction in the Columbia University neighborhood." In 1907, Charles Paterno established his own business, the Paterno Construction Company, with his brother-in-law Anthony Campagna. Working independently and in joint ventures, the members of the Paterno family built 37 apartment buildings on Morningside Heights, ranging from modest six-story structures to the impressive Luxor, Regnor, and Rexor on Broadway at 115th and 116th Streets and the Colosseum and Paterno on Riverside Drive and 116th Street. The Paternos were active during the entire span of apartment house development in the area, beginning with John Paterno's modest apartment buildings on 112th Street in 1898 and ending with Joseph Paterno's enormous 1924 building at 425 Riverside Drive. The Paterno's were so proud of their buildings that the facades of some of their grandest works are emblazoned with initials referring to the family: "P" for Paterno, "JP" for Joseph Paterno, or "PB" for Paterno Brothers. These initials often baffle modern viewers, but were probably recognized by many people at the time the buildings were erected, perhaps assuring potential renters that these were quality apartment houses.

The vast majority of other builders active in the Morningside Heights neighborhood were Jewish. Many were small-scale builders involved with only a few buildings, but others established major careers as apartment-house developers. Some built under their own names or as corporations that bore their names, but the most active Jewish builders incorporated as real estate firms with names stripped of Jewish ethnic identity. For example, Edgar A. Levy, Jacob Stein, and Leo S. Bing were partners in the Carlyle Realty Company, Jacob Axelrod was president of the West Side Construction Company, and Charles Newmark headed the Carnegie Construction Company.

Like the builders, many, but by no means all of the architects commissioned by the speculative developers to design apartment buildings were also from Italian and Jewish backgrounds, including Simon Schwartz, Arthur Gross, George and Edward Blum, Gaetan Ajello, and William Rouse. However, the builders did not necessarily hire architects of their own ethnic background. While Paterno Brothers commissioned three buildings from Italian architect Gaetan Ajello, the firm was most loyal to the Jewish architects Schwartz & Gross. The Jewish building company, B. Crystal and Son (incorporated by Bernard and Hyman Crystal), hired the Jewish architectural firm of George and Edward Blum for two buildings, but used Ajello for four additional structures, while the Jewish building firm West Side Construction almost always hired the non-Jewish architect George Pelham.

Andrew S. Dolkart continued,

> The architects who specialized in apartment-house design rarely trained at the leading architectural schools or apprenticed in prestigious offices. Rather, most were practitioners who, if they had any formal architectural training at all, had been educated in less prestigious offices or in technical schools. Since these

architects were not welcome in the higher echelons for the architectural profession because of their ethnic background and "inferior" training, they entered the field at the least prestigious end, designing speculative apartment houses. In fact, in the first decades of the twentieth century, few apartment house architects were members of the American Institute of Architects or the Architectural League of New York, bastions of the professional elite.

As a neighborhood that was part of the first wave of middle-class apartment-house construction in New York City, Morningside Heights contains an early concentration of speculative apartment buildings designed by these architects. Three firms, George Pelham, Neville and Bagge, and Schwartz & Gross, were responsible for more than half of the apartment houses on Morningside Heights and, indeed, for thousands of other apartment buildings located throughout Manhattan. Thus, they were among the most prolific designers ever to work in New York City. Although generally unheralded, it was Schwartz & Gross, George Pelham, Neville and Bagge, and other speculator architects who, by the sheer volume of their work, created the architectural character and texture of many of New York's neighborhoods, while more prestigious architects like McKim, Mead & White, Carrere and Hastings, and Delano and Aldrich designed only a small number of great monuments that are set amidst the city's more typical speculative buildings."

## Schwartz & Gross

New York Buildings

- 130 East 75th Street (1963)
- 1095 Park Avenue (1953)
- 180 East 79th Street (1930)
- 32 West 39th Street (1937)
- 113–15 East 72nd Street (1934)
- 116 West 72nd Street (1932)
- 99 Wall Street (1931)
- 241 Central Park West (1931)
- 14 Washington Place (1931)
- 55 Central Park West (1930)
- 44 Gramercy Park North (1930)
- 19 East 74th Street (1930)
- 101 Central Park West (1930)
- The Blakely New York at 136 West 55th Street (1930)
- 91 Central Park West (1929)
- 47–51 East 64th Street (1929)
- 30 East 72nd Street (1929)
- 30 East 71st Street (1929)
- 33 East 70th Street (1929)
- 325 East 57th Street (1929)
- 336 Central Park West (1929)
- 14 East 75th Street (1929)
- 1095 Park Avenue (1929)
- 1185 Park Avenue (1929)
- 410 East 57th Street (1929)
- 580 Eighth Avenue (1929)
- 40 East 72nd Street (1928)

- Hotel Lincoln a.k.a. The Milford Plaza at 700 8th Avenue (1928)
- 345 East 57th Street (1928)
- 113 East 78th Street (1928)
- 1040–1054 Lexington Avenue (1928)
- 1051 Lexington Avenue (1928)
- 175 East 79th Street (1928)
- 1070 Park Avenue (1928)
- Westover Apartments at 253 West 72nd Street (1928)
- 330 7th Avenue (1928)
- 440 West End Avenue (1928)
- Hotel Victoria (1928) *demolished*
- The Mark Hotel at 25 East 77th Street (1927)
- 885 Park Avenue (1927)
- 888 Park Avenue (1927)
- 20 East 76th Street (1926)
- 25 East 77th Street (1926)
- 30 East 72nd Street (1926)
- 983 Park Avenue (1926)
- Bricken Broadway Building at 1385 Broadway (1926)
- Court-Remsen Building at 26 Court Street in Downtown Brooklyn (1926)
- Pennsylvania Building a.k.a. 14 Penn Plaza at 225 West 34th Street (1925)
- 23 East 74th Street (1925)
- 111–113 East 75th Street (1925)
- 168–172 East 74th Street (1925)
- 912 Fifth Avenue (1925)
- 890 West End Avenue (1925)
- 37 Riverside Drive (1924)
- 30 Fifth Avenue (1923)

- 105 East 63rd Street (1922)
- 1 Harrison Street (1919)
- 70 East 77th Street (1917)
- Colonial Parkway Apartments at 409 Edgecombe Avenue (1917)
- Paul Robeson Residence a.k.a. Roger Morris at 555 Edgecombe Avenue (1916)
- 470 Park Avenue (1916)
- 1000 Madison Avenue (neo-federal façade added) (1916)
- 930 Park Avenue (1915)
- 525 Park Avenue (1914)
- Victoria Building at 230 Fifth Avenue (1914)
- 212 Fifth Avenue (1913)
- 315 Central Park West (1913)
- 111 West 71st Street (1913)
- 970 Park Avenue (1912)
- 12 West 17th Street (1912)
- 49 West Twenty-Third Street (1912)
- Craftsman Building at 6 East 39th (1912)
- The Grinnell at 800 Riverside Drive (1911)
- 6 West 18th Street (1910)
- The Colosseum Apartments at 435 Riverside Drive (1910)
- The Strachmore at 404 Riverside Drive (1909)
- The Paterno at 440 Riverside Drive (1909)
- 606 West 116th Street (1908)
- 610 West 116th Street (1908)
- 10 East 76th Street (1908)

# Chapter 7

## Sugarman & Berger

Morris Henry Sugarman (1889–1946) was born in Odessa and was educated as an immigrant in the public schools of New York. He studied at the National Academy of Design at Columbia University and abroad in England and France. He organized the architectural firm Sugarman & Berger in 1926.

Albert C. Berger (1879–1940) was born in Hungary. After studying technical education at the University of Budapest, Albert migrated to the United States in 1904. He began his career in New York as a draftsman employed in the office of Schwartz & Green and later spent several years with the firm of Starret and Van Vleck. After 1926, he was active in the firm of Sugarman & Berger until the end of his career in 1940.

Sugarman & Berger designed the historic forty-three-story New Yorker Hotel in 1930. Located at Thirty-Fourth Street at Eighth Avenue with 2,503 guest rooms, it was one of the city's largest hotels. Hotel management pioneer Ralph Hitz was selected as its first manager, eventually becoming president of the National Hotel Management Company. An early ad for the hotel boasted that the bell boys were "as snappy-looking, as West Pointers" and that the hotel had a radio in every room "with a choice of four stations." A New Yorker bellboy, Johnny Roventine, served as the tobacco company Philip Morris's pitchman for twenty years, making famous their "call for Philip Morris" advertising campaign.

Much like the Chrysler Building (1930) and the Empire State Building (1931), the New Yorker Hotel was designed in the Art Deco style. In his book *New York 1930*, Robert A. M. Stern wrote that:

> The New Yorker's virtually unornamented facades consisted of alternating vertical bands of warm grey brick and windows, yielding an impression of boldly modeled masses. This was furthered by the deep-cut light courts, which produced a powerful play of light and shade that was enhanced by dramatic lighting at night.

A 1938 brochure for the New Yorker Hotel described Manhattan's largest and tallest hotel as follows:

> A vertical village, where every vote of the citizens sends two thousand servants scurrying to satisfy their daily whims, is making history in the heart of New York. This town, which rises instead of spreads, reaches 43 stories toward the skies at Thirty-fourth Street and Eighth Avenue—The New Yorker, Manhattan's largest and tallest hotel. The New Yorker is a vertical city, for without stretching a point to make a phrase, it includes everything that any town has—and in many aspects, much more.

> Bellmen smart as West Pointers on parade reach for your bags when you enter the lobby through the tunnel from the Pennsylvania station or step off

the B. and O. railroad motor coach at the door. In this great hospitable lobby you immediately sense the luxury and completeness of New York's biggest hotel. Everything moves swiftly and smoothly, without friction or flurry twenty clerks are on duty at the huge front desk and it seems to be only a moment until you are registered and on the way to your room.

The season is the only limit on your appetite in the Terrace Restaurant, known in millions of homes throughout the United States through the four-night-a-week broadcasts over the nation-wide chains of a National Broadcasting Company. Its simple elegance makes it outstanding among dining salons. The superb service here is entirely a la carte, except at breakfast, when there is a seventy-five cent club meal, and at luncheon when club luncheons are featured at various prices. This restaurant is open again at six for breakfast.

World-famous orchestras interpret the syncopated rhythms of today nightly through the dinner hour and during supper in the Terrace Restaurant, except Sunday when there is dancing only at dinner. There is no cover at dinner; after ten o'clock at night it is one dollar except on Saturday and holidays when it is two. A concert orchestra plays during luncheon. Made-to-order weather cools this room, as it does all the other New Yorker restaurants and public rooms, so on even the hottest days of summer you can dine and dance without the slightest degree of discomfort.

The Manhattan Room is a delightfully informal restaurant, opening off the main lobby, where the matchless quality of the food is equaled only by the swift, unobtrusive service. Here, also, you find that elusive modern note characteristic of The New Yorker. The walls are built of Persian Walnut, inlaid with solid bronze, and the windows, facing Thirty-fourth Street, are notable for the exquisite craftmanship of their carved glass. Prices are reasonable with club dinners at $1.50 to $2.00 and luncheons at 75 cents to $1.25.

Down in great kitchens that cover an acre of floor space, one hundred and thirty-five of the world's most famous cooks have dedicated their lives to the service of your appetite. Here is delivered each day the choice of the world's finest food products to be made into palate-pleasing delights for the 10,000 appetites which daily endorse The New Yorker's cuisine. Even the breads, pastries and ice creams are made by our chefs, in these kitchens that are as sweet and clean as mother's cookie jar.

In the Empire Tea Room there is all the grace and charm of France under the Napoleonic era which inspired its green and gold decorations. Bright-faced girls in quaint French provincial costumes serve you breakfast, luncheon, dinner or supper. Here there is a soda fountain and here, too, is the New Yorker Candy Shop where you will find New Yorker Bonbonettes, the delicious new French candies. Food prices are reasonable-breakfast 35 cents and up; luncheon 75 cents; dinner one dollar; supper a la carte. Quick counter service is provided for you in the Coffee Shop, located in the lower lobby. It is open until nine o'clock each night. Breakfast is a la carte; luncheon is 60 cents and dinner is 90 cents. In the Coffee Shop, the food is served in all the delicious variety of the other three restaurants, for regardless of what you pay or in what restaurant you dine at The New Yorker you are assured of the same high quality and wholesome flavor. The Coffee Shop has an entrance to Eighth Avenue as well as a lobby entrance.

Twenty-three elevators, speeding at 800 feet a minute, travel 900 miles a day to carry you up to your room. All are self-leveling and automatic and they represent an investment of three-quarters of a million dollars. Operating at fully capacity they could transport the entire population of a city of 200,000 people in twenty-four hours. A special elevator serves the four function floors and another special elevator connects the lobby to the Pennsylvania station tunnel and to the new Eighth Avenue subway express when completed.

Priceless murals, gold-illumined ceilings, carved glass and inlaid Persian walnut have been deftly adapted for the modern setting of the Grand Ballroom. The foyer opens into the lobby mezzanine and a grand staircase connects it conveniently to the lobby itself. The Grand Ballroom accommodates 800 at a luncheon or diner and 1000 for dance or meeting. The balcony is accessible from both the ballroom floor and the function lounges on the third floor. The ballroom and other public rooms are air-cooled in summer.

Modern beauty and luxurious appointments distinguish the lounges and foyers. The very mode of the moment is mirrored in the striking decorations which reflect all the spirit and smartness of today. The spacious ballroom foyer on the second floor is decorated with murals by Louis Jambor, who also painted the murals for quiet corners with restful chairs and deep, comfortable divans where you may meet your friends.

The North Ballroom conveys an atmosphere of formal elegance. Essentially in the modern note it is a perfect locale for either social or business occasions. It accommodates three hundred and thirty persons for a luncheon or dinner and four hundred at a dance or meeting. Special service kitchens provide quick, flawless service to the two ballrooms. The North Ballroom also is air-cooled and is quickly accessible from the lobby by a grand stairway and the lobby mezzanine. It also is served by the special function elevator from the Thirty-fifth street entrance of the Hotel.

The ten private dining salons, located conveniently on the third and fourth floors, accommodate from twenty-five to one hundred and fifty persons for a meeting; luncheon, dinner or dance. The private dining rooms also are served by the special function elevator and are connected with special banquet kitchens to provide quick, smooth service. The decorations have been carried out in varied period motifs and the furnishings are striking examples of contemporary beauty and luxury. Every bedroom has a radio loud speaker with a choice of four programs; both tub and shower bath; Servidor; circulating ice water; hand telephone; bed-head; reading lamps; full-length mirror and full-sized beds. Every room has two or more windows and all rooms are outside and flooded with light and air. Floor secretaries on each floor take your messages when you are out and prevent the annoyance of standing in crowded lines in the lobby to receive your mail and keys.

The New Yorker has more than one hundred suites consisting of a parlor and one bedroom or a parlor and two bedrooms. The parlors have radio and Servidor. Some have disappearing beds and an extra bath. Others have private sky-terraces or roof gardens. Suites are available for as little as eleven dollars a day. Bedroom rates start at $3.50 a day for one person; $5.00 a day and up for two persons with double bed; and $5.50 a day up to two persons with twin beds. Rates are fixed and are posted in each room.

Bathrooms are marvels of modern beauty and convenience. The walls are finished in black and sea-green tiling and the fixtures are in chromium nickel. The towel racks above the medicine cabinet are generously filled with extra large bath, face and hand towels and a special radiator keeps the room comfortably warm in the winter. There is a double socket bedside the mirror to connect curling irons or massage machine.

Many suites open into sky-terraces where you can literally say "Good morning, Mr. Sun!" from these private roof gardens the whole vivid, far-flung panorama of New York lies at your feet in an animated tapestry of magic color and up here, a tenth of a mile above the street, you seem to be in a world apart. Far below you the lights of Times Square paint the darkness with splashes of flame and the Hudson cuts through the twilight haze like a silver ribbon. Room service will serve your dinner on your terrace if you wish.

The exquisite luxury and the compelling beauty of the ladies' lounge on the third floor are delightfully refreshing. An unusual feature is a series of tiny "powdering rooms" where milady, assisted by specially-trained French maids, can apply her cosmetics with the same privacy she finds in her our boudoir, and here also is a commodious checkroom for ladies attending functions in the ballrooms and dining salons and adjoining it is one of the famous Terminal Beauty Salons. The public stenographer's office is outside.

The beauty salon is truly a dream of green and orchid and silver. Walls of mosaic tiles in mauve and ivory and blue! Curtains of apple green shot with gleaming silver ivory chairs smartly upholstered in shiny patent black leather. And throughout this salon you will find the smooth perfection and correctness of service that characterizes truly authentic fashion. A shampoo? A wave? A facial? Each takes on a thrilling new loveliness under the skilled fingers of any of the thirty-two attendants. Open from nine a.m. till seven p.m.

And here is the largest barber shop in the world! Forty-two chairs and twenty manicurists. Seldom do you have to wait here, but if you want to be sure to have a barber ready for you, make an appointment by telephone from your room. The shop is operated by the Terminal Barber Shops, Inc., whose twenty years of experience in the nation's greatest cities enable them to perform the ten-point Terminal promise of the most perfect and hygienic standards in modern barbering practice. The shop is located in the lower lobby.

A quarter of a million-dollar radio system gives you entertainment and diversion in your room at the turn of a dial. The elaborate receiving apparatus, containing seventy-two tubes, give you a choice of four programs. Special apparatus enables us to bring you programs from foreign countries. Twenty-five miles of wires carry the programs to the 2500 loudspeakers in the rooms and to the amplifies in the ballrooms, private dining salons and other public rooms. The volume of sound from the speakers is automatically controlled to prevent guests from being annoyed by noise.

The New Yorker's private laundry with its one hundred and fifty employees and half-million dollars worth of machinery is capable of handling the entire family washing and ironing of a city of thirty thousand. It not only launders the thirty-two acres of sheets, the sixty-five miles of toweling and the other three hundred thousand pieces of linen used in the hotel, but a special guest department enables you to have your own laundry back in your room before six o'clock at night if the laundry receives it before ten in the morning. The valet department gives you half-hour service on pressing night and day.

Seventy-eight feet below the sidewalk is the largest private power plant in the world. Five steam engines and oil-burning Diesel engine produce enough light, heat, power and refrigeration for the average city of thirty-five thousand people. Compressed air forces pulverized coal under the furnaces and blows the ashes out again. The engineering equipment includes the air-cleaning machinery which draws in air on the roof, washes and purifies it, and then forces down into the restaurant, lobby, ballrooms and other public spaces.

The nimble fingers and quick minds of ninety-five telephone operators handle ninety-one incoming trunk lines, thirty-eight outgoing trunk lines and ten direct long-distance trunk lines in the huge telephone exchange on the forty-first floor. The system includes thirty-two hundred phones. In addition to this tremendous you in your absence from your room are taken by floor secretaries.

Located at Thirty-fourth Street and Eighth Avenue, The New Yorker is quickly accessible from the Holland Tunnel and the Jersey Tubes. A tunnel connects it to the Pennsylvania and Long Island trains and I.R.T. subways systems. When the new Eighth Avenue subway is completed in 1931 there will be express station almost within the hotel. The theatrical district and smart shops are a stone's throw away; the important piers nearby.

Almost every other service or convenience is found within the four walls of The New Yorker. A ten-room hospital on the fourth floor is open night and day; a theater ticket office buys amusement tickets at legal rates; the transportation department obtains your steamship, airways and railroad tickets; the flower shop and candy shop will deliver gifts anywhere; and for your convenience there are several shops on the lobby floor.

The New Yorker guests had direct access to Penn Station by means of the hotel's private tunnel. In 1939, NBC began broadcasting live from the Terrace Room, which became known for big band acts, as well as nightly ice-skating shows on the hotel's retractable ice-skating rink.

Throughout the 1940s and 1950s, the hotel was among New York's most fashionable. In the building's heyday. It hosted many popular big bands, such as Benny Goodman, Woody Herman, and Tommy Dorsey, while notable figures such as Spencer Tracy, Joan Crawford, and Fidel Castro stayed there. Inventor Nikola Tesla spent the last ten years of his life in near-seclusion in Suite 3327, where he died, largely devoting his time to feeding pigeons while occasionally meeting dignitaries. In later years, Muhammad Ali would recuperate there after his March 1971 fight against Joe Frazier at Madison Square Garden.

Notwithstanding its early success, New York's changing economy and demographics caused the New Yorker Hotel to slowly decline, and as a result, its ownership changed several times. It was purchased by Hilton Hotels in 1953 for $12.5 million and following an antitrust suit by the federal government, was sold three years later for $20 million to Massaglia Hotels. In 1959, Massaglia sold the hotel to an investment syndicate known as New York Towers Ltd., which went bankrupt, allowing Hilton to reacquire the building in 1967.

By the time Hilton reacquired the hotel, the pronounced decline in New York's economic fortunes, coupled with the construction of new, more modern hotels, caused the New Yorker to become unprofitable. As a result, Hilton closed the hotel in April 1972. Ultimately, in 1975, it was purchased by the Unification Church of the United States for $5.6 million. The church converted much of the building for use by its members. The hotel housed offices of many church departments and was known as the "World Mission Center" for several years. Church holy day celebrations were held there, with Sun Myung Moon often speaking to members in the Grand Ballroom. He also held "matchings" there, the first step in arranged marriages where he would suggest marriage partners to members who had gathered to be introduced to their future spouse. A notable example took place in 1982 when, following a matching ceremony, the newly engaged couples, joined by others who had been engaged two or three years previously, gathered in the New Yorker Hotel and walked across to Madison Square Garden to participate in the 2,075 couples marriage Blessing Ceremony.

In 1994, the Unification Church elected to convert a portion of the building to use as a commercial hotel again, and the New Yorker Hotel Management Company took over operation of the building. It began the largest renovation project in the New Yorker's nearly sixty-five-year history, completed in 1999, with $20 million in capital improvements. In 1997, the Tick Tock Diner opened on the corner of Thirty-Fourth Street and Eighth Avenue. With 280 seats, it claims to be the largest diner in New York City and serves meals around the clock.

The hotel joined the Ramada franchise chain in 2000. In August 2007, the hotel began a major capital improvement program, which was completed in February 2009 at a final cost of $70 million. These improvements increased the number of guest rooms available from 178 in 1994 to 912, located on floors 19 through 40.

The renovation project was designed by Stonehill and Taylor Architects. Interior improvements included room restructuring and augmentation (now called "Metro" and "City View" rooms). Other improvements included a refurbished front entrance, lobby redesign, foyer reconstruction, and ballroom renovations. The hotel also expanded its Wi-Fi and PDA support and added high-definition flat-screen televisions in all rooms. In addition, individual room air-conditioning units were replaced with modern centralized heating and cooling systems throughout the entire hotel. In 2009, conference room space was added to the hotel through the conversion of a defunct Manufacturer's Hanover Bank branch, bringing the total meeting space to just over thirty-three thousand square feet, including two ballrooms and twelve conference rooms.

The New Yorker Hotel joined the Wyndham Hotels chain in March 2014, which has undertaken additional upgrades to the hotel, including lobby and restaurant renovations, to attract more business travelers in anticipation of the massive Hudson Yards Redevelopment Project on the West Side of Manhattan.

## Other Sugarman & Berger Projects

1.  1 Fifth Avenue: Sugarman & Berger and Helms and Corbett designed the twenty-seven-story apartment hotel for developer Joseph S. Siegel. This was not a conventional apartment house but an apartment hotel of two- and three-room units, each with a serving pantry for food brought up by service elevator from a central restaurant on the ground floor. In fact, the apartment hotel was a widespread fiction of the period; "non-housekeeping" residential buildings could be built taller and deeper than regular multiple dwellings because they were considered commercial buildings—although some tenants set up full kitchens in the serving pantries.

In prior projects, builder Joseph Siegel had worked with the architects Sugarman & Berger, who produced standard-issue architecture. But for 1 Fifth Avenue, Siegel brought in Harvey Willy Corbett as design architect, perhaps because he had designed numerous highly regarded buildings for Sailor's Snug Harbor. Corbett was a free thinker in his architectural designs. He used shaded brick on the four turret-like corners and vertical, paired white and black brick stripes to imitate angled masonry projections rising between the windows.

The building is a visually stunning landmark that rarely goes unnoticed due to its imposing presence over Washington Square Park and as an anchor to Fifth Avenue. It gets high praise by tourists and natives because of its unique design amidst colorful Greenwich Village and the New York University campus. 1 Fifth Avenue features one hundred two-bedroom units, sixty one-bedroom units, and a few studios.

2. Gramercy Arms at 102 East Twenty-Second Street was designed by Sugarman & Berger and erected in 1928. The ninety-four-unit residential condominium building is notable for the attractive polychromatic glazed panels located below the second, fifth, seventh, and ninth floors and the even bolder three-story terra-cotta piers at its base.

3. The Broadway Fashion Building at 2315 Broadway was designed by Sugarman & Berger in 1931 as a four-story commercial building. Its Art Deco style and material gave this sleek structure a distinction that belies its modest size. The *AIA Guide to New York City Architecture* (Norval White and Elliot Willensky, 4th ed., 2000) describes its significance as follows:

> Long before the curtain walls of metal and glass descended upon midtown, this curtain wall of metal and glass and glazed terra-cotta came to grace Broadway.

Sugarman & Berger, prolific designers of both residential and commercial buildings throughout New York City, caught the critics attention with the Broadway Fashion Building. The *New York Times* commented that the "facades will be 90 percent glass, with white stainless metal for decorative work" in vivid contrast to neighboring buildings of solid masonry. The *Times* also noted that "a system of exterior and interior illumination will give the structure an unusual appearance at night." The building was intended to glow in the evening while during the day the nearly all-glass design allowed natural light to reach the high-end retail shops on each of the floors.

4. The Hotel Paris at Ninety-Seventh Street and West End Avenue was built as an inexpensive club for traveling salesmen (much like the YMCA). It had a rooftop solarium, a pool, and small guest rooms each with a private bath. In its declining years, the Paris attracted busloads of tourists on cheap package tours, like a hostel. The Paris became little better than an SRO (single-occupancy dwelling) or welfare hotel. By the 1980s, it was closed, renovated, and turned into luxury rentals.

In 2015, Bruce Menin of Crescent Heights sold it to Laurence Gluck of Stellar Management for $150 million.

5. Navarro Flats on Central Park South was twice the size of the Dakota Apartment and was developed by Jose Francisco de Navarro, the Spanish-born entrepreneur. His gigantic eight-building Navarro Flats complex was built in the 1880s and took up the westerly end of Central Park South bounded by Sixth and Seventh Avenues. The buildings, each thirteen stories tall, were named the Madrid, the Cordova, the Granada, the Valencia, the Lisbon, the Barcelona, the Saragosa, and

the Tolosa. The sales brochure for the apartments, most of them seven-bedroom duplexes, listed them at $20,000 for corner units and $15,000 for those with only one exposure. The architects, Sugarman & Berger and Hubert and Pirsson staggered the floors so that the principal rooms, facing the street, had extra-high ceilings.

Unlike the cool beige brick and stone of the Dakota, the Navarro Flats buildings were hot-red brick set off against a cliff of stone-trimmed arches, turrets, gables, and other features—an arrangement that *Scientific American* called "most unsatisfactory" in 1884. There were some Moorish details, but the buildings were also described as both Gothic and Queen Ann in style. The construction chronology is hazy, but it appears that the westernmost two buildings were completed in early 1884, the next two in 1885, and the last four several years after that.

Mr. de Navarro was regularly reported to be involved in lawsuits and troubled business affairs, but in 1884, he filed plans for apartment complexes at Eighty-Sixth Street and Madison Avenue, and at Eighty-First Street and Central Park West. That year, *The Record and Guide* said that the Navarro Flats "must have proved very profitable." By 1885, however, the publication reported that there had been few sales and that there was "little doubt that the venture will prove to be the reverse of profitable." The project required a second mortgage—and a third, which Mr. de Navarro could not get. The scent of failure was death to further sales or credit, and the mortgage holders were suing by 1886.

In November 1888, *The New York Daily Tribune* reported the cost of each building as $2 million, and the complex was sold at auction, with at least two of the buildings still incomplete. The original shareholders lost their equity—or, as *The Tribune* put it, they had bought only "castles in the air." The spectacular failure of the Navarro Flats put a damper on the nascent co-op movement, which suffered from its failure for years.

Not that any stigma attached itself to living at the Navarro Flats. In 1890, the writer and reformer Carl Schurz lived in the Lisbon; Mary Mapes Dodge, the author of *Hans Brinker, or The Silver Skates*, lived in the Cordova; and Percy Chubb, the insurance executive, lived in the Valencia.

Court battles relating to the project followed Mr. de Navarro at least to 1902, when disappointed stockholders won a suit against him for $950,000. That suggests he still had enough money to pay, and indeed in the mid-1880s, he had organized a successful cement company, which seems to have occupied much of his time until his death in 1909.

Beginning in 1926, Mr. de Navarro's towering vision was sold off and demolished. The apartment buildings were replaced by the New York Athletic Club, the Essex House, and the Hampshire House, leaving not a trace of the Navarro Flats.

# Chapter 8

## Frank Mills Andrews

Frank Mills Andrews (1867–1948) was a very prolific architect of the early twentieth century, yet his work goes largely unrecognized. He designed almost all of the National Cash Register buildings and the Hotel McAlpin, which was the tallest hotel in the world. He designed the Dayton Arcade, the Reibold Building, and the St. Henry's Memorial Chapel at Calvary Cemetery.

He was born in Des Moines, Iowa, on January 8, 1867. His father was Lorenzo Frank Andrews, and his mother was Sophia Maxwell Dolson.

Andrews studied civil engineering at Iowa State College and architecture at Cornell University and then trained in the office of William Miller, Ithaca, New York; worked for George B. Post, New York, followed by Jenney and Mundie, Chicago, Illinois from 1891 until 1893, including work on the World's Columbian Exposition.

When NCR President John Patterson attended the exposition and saw Andrews's ability to work with European styles, he asked him to come to Dayton, Ohio, to design buildings for the National Cash Register Company. Andrews operated from a headquarters atop the Conover Building, which he designed, in Dayton from

1893 until 1907, first with Charles I. Williams and then on his own. In the NCR projects, and the homes of a few significant Daytonians, he partnered with the Olmsted Brothers Landscape Company to create structures with visual continuity of interior and exterior beauty.

Andrews designed and oversaw construction of the St. Henry's Memorial Chapel at Calvary Cemetery in 1898 through its completion in 1902. The chapel was built as a memorial atop the mass grave of four thousand unidentified Civil War remains reinterred from St. Henry's, the original Catholic cemetery in Dayton. Andrews used the Victorian-Gothic style in this structure.

At Patterson's suggestion, Andrews designed the Dayton Arcade (1899) as a marketplace for the growing downtown area, to resemble a Dutch Guild Hall as he had done in the 1893 Columbian Exposition.

Andrews opened an office in Cincinnati and operated it from 1905 until 1908. Works in the Cincinnati area include the Hotel Sinton (1907) and renovation of the Gidding-Jenny Store (1910). Andrews was associated with Charles P. Taft of Cincinnati in these and other hotel developments: Hotel Sinclair in Cincinnati, Ohio; Hotel Taft in New Haven, Connecticut; Hotel McAlpin, Battle House Hotel in Mobile, Alabama; and the Battle Creek Sanitarium in Battle Creek, Michigan.

## Hotel McAlpin, New York, New York

The Hotel McAlpin was constructed in 1912 by General Edwin A. McAlpin, son of David Hunter McAlpin. As well as being the world's largest hotel, it was also one of the most luxurious. The amenities were as breathtaking as they were opulent, including a massive Turkish bath and plunge pool on the twenty-fourth floor. The hotel also had its own in-house orchestra and fully-equipped hospital.

When construction of the Hotel McAlpin neared completion by the end of 1912 as the largest hotel in the world, *The New York Times* commented that it was so tall at twenty-five stories that it "seems isolated from other buildings." Boasting a staff of 1,500, the hotel could accommodate 2,500 guests. It was built at a cost of $13.5 million ($358 million today). The hotel was designed by noted architect Frank Mills Andrews whose design included two gender-specific floors: women checking into the hotel could reserve a room on the women's-only floor, bypass the lobby, and check in directly on their own floor. Another floor, dubbed the "sleepy sixteenth," was designed for night workers and was kept quiet during the day. The hotel also had its own travel agency.

The McAlpin underwent an expansion half a decade later. The owners had purchased an additional fifty feet of frontage on Thirty-Fourth Street two years earlier. The new addition was the same height as the original twenty-five-story building and provided an additional two hundred rooms, four more elevators, and a large ballroom. A major refurbishment, costing $2.1 million, was completed in 1928, refreshing all the rooms, installing modern bathrooms, and updating the elevators.

The McAlpin family sold the hotel in 1938 to Jamlee Hotels, headed by Joseph Levy, president of Crawford Clothes, a prominent real estate investor in New York for $5.400,000. Jamlee reportedly invested an additional $1,760,000 in renovations. During the Jamlee ownership, the hotel was managed by the Knott Hotel Company until 1952 when management was taken over by the

Tisch Hotel Company. On October 15, 1954, Jamlee sold the hotel to the Sheraton Hotel Corporation for $9,000,000 and it was renamed the Sheraton-McAlpin. Sheraton completely renovated the hotel five years later and renamed it the Sheraton-Atlantic Hotel on October 8, 1959. Sheraton sold the hotel to the investing partnership of Sol Goldman and Alexander DiLorenzo on July 28, 1968 for $7.5 million, and it reverted to the Hotel McAlpin name. Sheraton briefly reacquired the hotel in 1976, through a default by the buyers, and quickly sold it to developer William Zeckendorf Jr. who converted the McAlpin to seven hundred rental apartments and named it the Herald Square Apartments.

On Christmas Eve 1916, Harry K. Thaw, former husband of Evelyn Nesbit and the murderer of architect Stanford White, attacked nineteen-year-old Fred Gump Jr. in a large suite on the eighteenth floor. Thaw had enticed Gump to New York with a promise of a job but instead sexually assaulted him and beat him repeatedly with a stocky whip until he was covered in blood. According to the *New York Times*, Thaw had rented two rooms on either side of his suite to muffle the screams. The next day, Thaw's bodyguard took Gump to the aquarium and zoo before the boy managed to escape. Gump's father sued Thaw for $650,000 for the "gross indignities" that his son suffered. The case was eventually settled out of court.

In 1920, the McAlpin Hotel hosted what may have been the first broadcast from a New York hotel. The Army Signal Corps arranged the broadcast by singer Luisa Tetrazzini from her room in the hotel. Tetrazzini (1871–1940) was an Italian lyric coloratura soprano who had an enormous popularity in America from the 1900s until the 1920s. In 1922, the McAlpin became one of the first hotels to link ship-to-shore radios with its phone system. The hotel would later be the first to give the call letters of radio station WMCA in 1925.

In 1947, Jackie Robinson, a resident living on the eleventh floor, received the phone call from the Brooklyn Dodgers that would change America forever by becoming the first African American player on a Major League Baseball team.

The hotel's Marine Grill was considered one of the more unusual interiors in the city of New York due to "an expansive grotto of exquisite polychrome terra-cotta designed by artist Frederick Dana Marsh." In the 1970s, the building owner had closed the restaurant, and historic preservationists were concerned with the future of the artwork. Their worst fears were realized when Susan Tunick, president of the nonprofit Friends of Terra Cotta, saw dumpsters outside the hotel filled with fragments from the murals. Rescue efforts were eventually successful when the murals were reassembled under the oversight of the MTA Arts for Transit Program, and they were reassembled piece by piece like a giant jigsaw puzzle over one summer by a group of college interns. In 2000, the restored murals were installed at the Fulton Street Station, along with the ornate iron gate that had adorned the entrance to the Marine Grill.

## George Washington Hotel, New York, New York

The George Washington Hotel in New York City's Gramercy Park District was designed by architect Frank Mills Andrews and opened in 1928. At different times, it has been used both as a brothel and as a bootlegging house during Prohibition. In 1939, the poet W. H. Auden stayed at the hotel, calling it "the nicest hotel in town," and another famous resident was writer Christopher Isherwood.

The George Washington Hotel, located at 23 Lexington Avenue, has been occupied by many famous writers, musicians, and poets, including Keith Haring who lived in the building as a student at the School of Visual Arts.

In the 1980s, the hotel was raided by the police. For a period of time, the building was in receivership; its demolition was prevented by support from a local historical society. The hotel was later purchased at auction, and space was leased to the not-for-profit Educational Housing Services in the mid-1990s during the city's rebirth. Much of the space was under sublease to the School of Visual Arts except for apartments still occupied by original tenants who paid stabilized rent—and who are still protected under New York City's rent laws. SVA broke the sublease and built a new dorm on Twenty-Fourth street in 2016. The ground lease for the property was bought by the investment firm Alliance Bernstein in 2016.

This historic building in Manhattan's Flatiron District that was once home to the famous George Washington Hotel (and to some of the most prominent artists and writers of the past century) is now the newest outpost of the Freehand Hotel collection. Designed by Roman and Williams in collaboration with the Sydell Group, Freehand/New York has 395 rooms, two restaurants, and a bar with an old-school New York flair. The team took care to restore the building's interiors while modernizing them with commissioned murals in partnership with artists from Bard College, plus a mix of vintage and custom-made furniture. The result? A new breath of life for this ninety-year-old building.

# The Battle House Hotel, Mobile, Alabama

The hotel is now known as the Battle House Renaissance Mobile Hotel. It was built in 1908 and replaced an earlier hotel that opened in 1852 and burned down in 1905. It was built by James Battle and his two half nephews on the site of Andrew Jackson's military headquarters during the War of 1812. The first Battle House had famous guests such as Henry Clay, Jefferson Davis, Millard Fillmore, Winfield Scott, and Stephen A. Douglas on the night that he lost the presidency to Abraham Lincoln. After the 1905 fire, the owners hired architect Frank M. Andrews, and he designed a new structure built of steel and concrete, which opened in 1908.

President Woodrow Wilson was a guest in 1913 where he made his infamous statement that "the US would never again wage another war of aggression." The hotel was owned and operated by the Sheraton Corporation until it was closed in 1974.

In 2003, the Retirement Systems of Alabama began restoration of the hotel along with the construction of an adjoining skyscraper, the RSA Battle House Tower. Both buildings opened in May 11, 2007 with a gala celebration attended by six hundred guests.

Wikipedia described the renovated hotel as follows:

> The eight-story building is steel frame with marble and brick facings. The hotel lobby features a domed skylight, dating back to 1908. The ceiling and walls are finished with elaborate plasterwork and are also painted using the trompe-l'oeil technique. The walls are painted with portraits of Louis XIV of France, George III of the United Kingdom, Ferdinand V of Castile and George Washington.

The Trellis Room, Mobile's only Four-Diamond restaurant specializes in Northern Italian cuisine and features a full-view kitchen so patrons can watch the chefs prepare their meals. The Trellis Room ceiling contains a Tiffany glass skylight. The Crystal Ballroom is now used for social events such as parties, honorary dinners, weddings, meetings, and Mardi Gras balls.

In praise of Mobile's Mardi Gras history, a giant Moon Pie drops at midnight to ring in the New Year. Moon Pies are thrown from Mardi Gras floats each year and the giant confection replica is across the street from the Battle House.

In 2009, the Battle House was named "One of the Top 500 Hotels in the World" by *Travel and Leisure* Magazine. The Spa at the Battle House opened that same year. In 2010, the hotel became a member of the Historic Hotels of America, the official program of the National Trust for Historic Preservation.

## The Hotel Taft, New Haven, Connecticut

The corner of College and Chapel Streets in downtown New Haven has featured five taverns or hotels for the past three centuries. Hostelries or public houses have stood on this parcel of land, on the southwest corner of the New Haven Green, from colonial times to the present. The land was originally allotted to William Hawkins of London. When Mr. Hawkins did not immigrate to America, the lot was purchased by Deputy Governor (of New Haven Colony) Stephen Goodyear, who then built a mansion on it. After Goodyear's death, it was purchased by the innkeeper of the town, John Harriman, who operated an early seventeenth-century "ordinary" in the mansion. Ordinaries provided a complete meal and sleeping accommodations for one price. An ordinary was also licensed to draw wine and sell it for retail.

In 1909, the property was purchased by a corporation known as the New Haven Company, which erected the Hotel Taft in the colonial revival style, by a group of local investors and named after one of them, Horace Taft, who was the headmaster of the Taft School in Watertown, Connecticut. The Hotel Taft, designed by architect Frank Mills Andrews from New York, had a reputation throughout New England and beyond. Adjacent to Yale University and overlooking the picturesque New Haven Green, the Taft's location was considered ideal, in spite of the fact that it was some distance from the railroad station. It opened for business on January 1, 1912, as an ultra-modern, twelve-story building with 450 rooms. A grand lobby, stores, restaurants, and bars occupied the first two floors. A large ballroom took up the upper two floors. The lobby is actually a great rotunda complete with a balcony and a stained glass dome. To this day, the Corinthian-columned grand lobby is seventy feet tall and capped with a breathtaking stained glass, which is rumored to be the largest piece of its type to come from Tiffany's studio.

The Hotel Taft was the focal and meeting point for society and traveler alike—a symbol of the city's academic and cultural prominence. Up to one million visitors passed through its doors every year.

For eight years immediately following his presidency, William Howard Taft lived in the hotel that bears his family name while he taught constitutional law at Yale University. President Taft was the principal speaker at the chamber of commerce dinner on January 19, 1912.

One of its earliest notable guests was Woodrow Wilson, who visited on September 12, 1912 during a presidential campaign stop—the campaign in which he went on to defeat the incumbent, President Taft. Numerous secretaries of state and treasury, including Andrew William Mellon, Cordell Hull, and Henry Lewis Stimson also checked in at the Taft, as well as Vice President Calvin Coolidge, in 1921.

Prohibition in the United States took place from 1920 through 1933. During this time, a speakeasy was created in one of the basements of the Hotel Taft. President Taft was a staunch opponent of the amendment that prohibited alcohol. Therefore, it seems fitting that the hotel bearing his family name had such an establishment.

With the Shubert Theater as its next door neighbor, the Hotel Taft saw many famous personalities walk through its elegant entrance— or underground since there was a tunnel that connected each building in the basement. Countless runs of pre-Broadway shows were performed at the Shubert Theatre by the likes of Humphrey Bogart, Spencer Tracy, the Marx Brothers, W. C. Fields, Gloria Swanson, Mary Martin, Al Jolson, Eddie Cantor, Katherine Hepburn, Alec Guinness, Henry Fonda, Olivia de Havilland, George Arliss, Walter Hampden, Sarah Bernhardt, Margaret Sullavan, Chauncey Olcott, and John, Lionel, and Ethel Barrymore. Lorraine Hansberry stayed at the Hotel Taft when *A Raisin in the Sun* was beginning its trial run. It is purported that Groucho Marx used to begin his monologue by stating, "I got kicked out of the best hotel in the world, the Hotel Taft in New Haven."

Shows were premiered in New Haven rather than in New York City to avoid the embarrassment of a flop on Broadway, where it would garner more press. The producers of the time felt they could gauge a sophisticated Broadway audience's reaction by a New Haven reaction. The producers sent Rodgers and Hammerstein back to their rooms at the Taft to rewrite the showstopper "Oklahoma!" and a hit was born.

Over the years, Hotel Taft left its mark on popular culture. Cole Porter's tune "Antoinette Birby" recounts the exploits of two colorful waitresses at the Taft. Gary Trudeau included the Taft in a Doonesbury comic strip. At the request of Taft Management, the Yale a cappella group Out of the Blue wrote "Ride the Chariot" and performed the premiere in the grand lobby in order to celebrate the 1996 Taft Apartments passenger elevator modernization. Today, the Taft community can view the lyrics to the Porter tune, the Doonesbury comic strip, and the Out of the Blue original score on the memorabilia wall in the grand lobby.

Scenes of The Hotel Taft are memorialized in three classic movies: *All about Eve* (1950), *Death of a Scoundrel* (1956) and *Splendor in the Grass* (1961).

Stefan Zweig, the best-selling Austrian writer and playwright of the 1920s and 1930s, wrote pieces of his fascinating and brilliant autobiography, *The World of Yesterday,* at the Hotel Taft. The publisher's postscript states that: "Part of the book was sketched during his residence ... at the Taft Hotel, New Haven, where he sojourned for a period while toying with the thought of settling in the shadow of Yale University." Zweig's books, plays, and poems were translated into just about every language. He was a friend of every famous author and conductor and artist. The director Wes Anderson mentioned in the credits to his movie *The Grand Hotel Budapest* that he was inspired by Zweig's autobiography.

The Taft Apartments "starred" in the popular television series *Gilmore Girls*. With the collaboration of Taft Management, a Hollywood set was built based on an actual Taft apartment floor plan. The main character, Rory, was asked to move into her boyfriend Logan's apartment at the Taft after she was kicked out of her apartment by her roommate. Episode 14 of season 6, "You've Been Gilmored," originally aired on February 7, 2006. Logan's apartment had a recurring role for several episodes.

Albert Einstein, Admiral Richard Byrd, Mrs. Eleanor Roosevelt, Gustaf VI Adolf of Sweden, Bill Tilden, Jack Dempsey, Jim Londos, Strangler Lewis, Lou Gehrig, and Babe Ruth were just a few of the more prominent names to have stayed at Hotel Taft.

Without a doubt, the most popular guest was Babe Ruth. In 1932, the New York Yankees came to New Haven to play the local baseball club. An estimated ten thousand children were waiting outside the Hotel Taft for "the Babe." When his car drew up, youngsters crowded around and jumped on it. It broke down in the middle of the street. Police did all they could do to manage the crowd during his time in New Haven.

The Hotel Taft had a staff of three hundred men and women to cover all that its numerous guests would need. The main dining room, which seated three hundred, attracted approximately nine hundred people daily; the cocktail lounge that seated sixty usually served 150 a day, and the Tap Room, which accommodated another sixty, took care of two hundred more visitors daily. Meanwhile, a barbershop, newsstand, and tobacco shop attracted other patrons.

The Hotel Taft was both a public and private success. While keeping occupancy rates high, it also provided public benefit to the city: prestige, architectural beauty, a meeting place, a site for Yale events, and a generator of spillover business by housing a pharmacy, newsstand, florists, and other small services. Most importantly, the Hotel Taft managed to do all of this in the face of some of the most trying economic circumstances the United States had seen—from the end of World War I until after the end of the Great Depression—and without government support.

All the while, the Hotel Taft never lost sight of customer service. Several quotes from Robert Richardson, a desk clerk for more than forty years, include "a good hotel employee tries to keep his personality out of it. He is a part of a smoothly working machine and if he has the hotel's interests at heart, he will do this job as quietly and unobtrusively as possible," and "today's guests demand courtesy and efficient service and that's what we try to give them."

Managers at the Hotel Taft were known to be inventive and were written up in numerous articles in the *New York Times*. In one instance, utilizing his expertise in food service, hospitality, and efficiency, former Hotel Taft manager J. C. La Vin was noted in an October 7, 1917 *New York Times* article as having invented a motorized kitchen that was capable of serving up to six thousand meals per day for soldiers on the march. The invention was named the "Taft Army Field Kitchen." Previous methods of feeding a large volume of moving soldiers were considered inefficient and unsanitary. Mr. La Vin's son, Craig La Vin, was also a former hotel manager. When the younger Mr. La Vin noticed that business in the dining room was slow, he installed an attractive cocktail lounge to rejuvenate business, which proved to be successful. The Tap Room was also built under his direction and is among his notable contributions.

The Hotel Taft thrived until 1945 when an increase in automobile travel and new interstate highways spurred the building of new hotels in surrounding areas. The Wilbur Cross Parkway, opened in 1950, and the Connecticut Turnpike, opened in 1959, struck a devastating blow to The Taft. Adding to the problem was the decline in train travel, something the Taft relied on heavily for guests. Lack of parking near the Taft forced lodgers to seek more convenient locations. Mayor Richard C. Lee's redevelopment of downtown New Haven brought another hotel to New Haven in 1970, the Sheraton Park Plaza, located just one block from the Taft. With only enough business to support one large downtown hotel, the Hotel Taft was forced to close its doors in October 1973.

Vacant from 1973 until 1981, the Taft was converted into apartments by the Starrett Housing Corporation of New York. Taft Realty Associates, LLC purchased the property on September 8, 1995, and the current management team has been in place since 1994. Since the mid 1990s, the Taft has seen extensive cosmetic and structural projects that continue to preserve and update the real estate. While fully embracing its rich history, as the building turned one hundred years old on January 1, 2012, the Taft team has a reputation of appreciating yesterday's laurels—but never staying sedentary.

## The Claypool Hotel, Indianapolis, Indiana

After its opening in 1903, the Claypool Hotel was the superstar for decades. It was built in 1903 by Edward F. Claypool and Henry W. Lawrence to designs by architect Frank Mills Andrews. The building was almost like a city unto itself with an electric light plant, waterworks facility, fire protection system, pumping station, steam laundry, mechanical refrigeration system, ice-making plant, Turkish bath, swimming pool, and barber shop.

The first big event at the hotel was the music recital by the famous German contralto Madam Schumann-Heink. The large audience of music lovers left the assembly room at the end of the concert in such a happy frame of mind that nobody seemed to object to trudging down eight flights of stairs to the ground floor because only one elevator was in working order.

The Claypool Hotel expanded in 1914 from four hundred to six hundred guest rooms and served the city as one of its most beloved venues until a 1967 fire. Despite the Claypool's ads which noted "absolutely fireproof," the hotel was so badly damaged in the fire that it was demolished in 1969.

## The Seelbach Hotel, Louisville, Kentucky

The Seelbach Hotel is an historic property in Louisville, Kentucky, founded by Bavarian-born immigrant brothers Louis and Otto Seelbach. They emigrated from Frankenthal, Germany, a small, rural town in Bavaria. Louis Seelbach arrived in Louisville in 1869 at age seventeen, shortly after reaching the United States. He worked in the first Galt House for a time upon his arrival, but after turning twenty-two in 1874, he realized he had greater ambitions.

He opened the Seelbach Bar and Grill that same year, and quickly built it into a flourishing enterprise. The success of the restaurant in Louisville's quickly expanding population and economy allowed Louis Seelbach to bring his brother Otto from Germany to help open the first Seelbach Hotel in 1891 above the bar and grill on Sixth and Main. The brothers were intent on building Louisville's first grand hotel: a hotel reflecting the opulence of European hotels. They purchased a piece of property at the corner of Fourth and Walnut (now Muhammad Ali Boulevard). Streets broke ground in December 1903 and opened its doors on May 1, 1905, just in time for the Kentucky Derby.

On the opening day, more than twenty-five thousand people visited the hotel. The Seelbach hosted a gala that evening, with dinner parties in each of the 150 rooms. The structure incorporated marble from Italy, Germany, and France, along with wood from the West Indies and Europe.

The hotel attracted large numbers of patrons in its first two years, and, luckily, the Seelbach Realty Company—formed in 1902 before the property purchase—had been planning from opening day to expand the hotel. On January 1, 1907, the second phase opened, raising the number of rooms to five hundred. The lower two floors of the ten-story structure were faced with stone, and the upper floors were brick. The rooftop garden was enclosed to allow it to be used as a winter garden.

At the time of construction, little else existed in the area around Fourth and Walnut Streets. When the Seelbach brothers proposed their project, the mayor of Louisville said, "No one will come to a hotel so far away." Several others attempted to discourage building on property so far from the "center" of Louisville. Since then,

Louisville has expanded—and the Seelbach Hotel has long been astride one of the city's booming shopping and business districts. Between the 1930s and 1960s, the Seelbach Hotel even anchored an area with Louisville's shops. Although it fell into disrepair for a time, today the area is again a bustling cultural and commercial center. Not only has the city grown around the hotel, but more hotel owners were inspired to build in the same area after seeing the Seelbach's success.

In 1925, when Louis Seelbach, president of the Seelbach Hotel Co., died, Chicago-based businessman Abraham M. Liebling bought the hotel for approximately $2.5 million. In 1929, he sold the hotel to the Eppley Hotel Company for $2 million. Mr. Eppley, of Omaha, Nebraska, owned many hotels throughout the Midwest, but he eventually sold the Seelbach Hotel and all his other properties in 1956 to Sheraton as part of a $30 million deal. This made the Seelbach part of the second largest hotel sale in US history. The hotel became the Sheraton-Seelbach Hotel, but its name was soon shortened to just the Sheraton Hotel. Sheraton sold the property to Gotham Hotels in 1968, and it regained the Seelbach name. Following a severe national economic slump in 1975, it closed after the owners went bankrupt.

In 1978, Louisville native and Hollywood television actor, Roger Davis, bought the Seelbach. Restoration work began in early 1979 and continued until the grand reopening on April 12, 1982. National Hotels Corporation, a subsidiary of Radisson Hotels and DoubleTree Hotels managed of the property, which had regained much of its former reputation.

The hotel has changed hands a number of times and when MeriStar Hospitality Corp bought the hotel in 1998, it became the Seelbach

Hilton. By 2009, it was jointly owned by Interstate Hotels and Resorts and Investcorp and operating under the Hilton flag. In 2009, the hotel completed a renovation at a cost of $12 million.

Restaurants in the Seelbach include the Oakroom, Gatsby's on Fourth, and Starbucks. The Oakroom is Kentucky's only AAA Five Diamond Restaurant Award winner, one of only forty-four in the nation, and the Rathskeller, decorated with Rookwood pottery, was a rare and distinctively Seelbach south-German influenced restaurant. The German term "Rathskeller" means "council's cellar" and is a common name in German-speaking countries that refers to a bar or restaurant located in the basement of a city hall.

Many American presidents have chosen to spend time at the hotel while in Louisville, including William Howard Taft (1911), Woodrow Wilson (1916), Franklin D. Roosevelt (1938), Harry Truman (1948), John F. Kennedy (1962), Lyndon B. Johnson (1964), Jimmy Carter (1970s), Bill Clinton (1998), and George W. Bush (2002).

The Rolling Stones, Whitney Houston, Elvis Presley, Billy Joel, Robin Williams, Russell Crowe, Julia Child, Wolfgang Puck, and Shorty Rossi, reality TV personality of Pit Boss, are among those celebrities who have stayed at the Seelbach.

F. Scott Fitzgerald frequented the hotel in April 1918, while training for his deployment in World War I. One night, after expensive bourbon and cigars, he had to be restrained and was rejected from the hotel. This experience seemingly did not tarnish his memories however, as he later included a fictional hotel akin to the Seelbach as the setting for the wedding of Tom and Daisy Buchanan in *The Great Gatsby*. In this story, it is referenced that Tom "rented out an entire floor of the Mulbach hotel," which could either refer to the Grand Ballroom (once located on the roof of the hotel) or the Rathskeller room (located in the basement) where Fitzgerald often went to the bar.

Lucky Luciano, Dutch Schultz, and Al Capone—who was a frequent guest of the Seelbach—stayed at the hotel, often for clandestine poker games. One story from the 1920s involves Al Capone sneaking out through a series of secret stairways and tunnels when Louisville Police broke up one of these games. Hotel staff are frequently eager to show the Al Capone room and give its history.

In February 2020, it was announced that the Seelbach Hotel filed an application with the city to build an eleven-story tower on the north side of the existing Seelbach annex wing and above an existing two-story ballroom addition. In a statement, Rockbridge, the Columbus, Ohio-based investment firm that bought the hotel two years ago, said the upgrade also will include a "comprehensive renovation" of all existing guest rooms and public spaces. "This will be a transformational project for both the city of Louisville and the state of Kentucky," Jim Merkel, Rockbridge's chief executive, said in the release. "By reestablishing the iconic nature of this historic hotel, we will shine national attention on Louisville and Kentucky."

The 150-foot tower will include guest rooms between the second and ninth floors, a meeting space at the tenth floor, and a rooftop bar, which will have both an indoor and an outdoor space, according to the application. All told, the addition will include a little more than thirty thousand square feet, expanding the facility to a 300,000-square-foot, 308-room hotel.

To stay competitive, some of the city's biggest downtown properties, including the Galt House and the Louisville Marriott, have announced renovations of more than $100 million combined.

CBRE Hotels Americas Research reported nearly a year ago that Louisville led the nation with a quarterly increase of 11.4 percent in demand for hotel rooms. That number was higher than many other cities because of pent-up demand for rooms while the Kentucky International Convention Center was shut down for renovations and the period leading up to the opening of 612-room Omni Hotel in 2018.

Rockridge, which specializes in real estate, announced in December 2017 that it had acquired the Seelbach and had enlisted Musselman Hotels in Louisville as the property's management team. The reported purchase price by RB Seelbach LLC was $38.6 million. Chester Musselman, president and CEO of Musselman Hotels, said his company has "a track record of executing comprehensive projects like the Seelbach, and when done, we will deliver a hotel commensurate with the legacy and history of the storied Seelbach."

Late in his career, architect Frank Mills Andrews partnered with H. E. Kennedy and J. S. Adkins in New York City from 1910 until 1914. As part of World War I, he extended his scope of construction to England and began designing buildings throughout the world. Andrews resumed his American career in architecture in 1929 before the stock market crash.

Andrews was elected a member of the Royal Society of Arts, London, to which he presented a paper in the Beaux Arts Influence on Architecture in America, which earned him their top prize in 1907.

A dashingly handsome man, Andrews married the glamorous screen actress Pauline Frederick in 1909. They had a daughter. After a messy divorce, Andrews married Ellen Brown in 1927. Their children included two daughters, Doris and Audrey, and one son, Frank Mills Andrews II.

Andrews died September 3, 1948 in Brooklyn, New York.

# Chapter 9

## Murgatroyd & Ogden

Everett Frederick Murgatroyd (1880–1946) was born in New York City and was trained as a civil engineer. Prior to his partnership with Palmer Ogden, he was an architect of factories in the Bronx. Palmer Harmon Ogden (1881–1959) was born in Dutchess County, New York. He graduated from Cooper Union in 1906.

In 1922, Murgatroyd & Ogden formed their partnership and became the corporate architects for the Allerton Hotel chain. They collaborated with Arthur Loomis Harmon, the Allerton's consulting architect, and partnered with other architects for out-of-town commissions. Their connection in Chicago was the architectural firm of Fugard and Knapp. In addition to their very successful work for the Allerton Hotels, Murgatroyd & Ogden received commissions from James S. Cushman, William Silk, the Salvation Army, and financier Bernard Baruch.

Their work for the Allerton Company included the Allerton Hotel in Cleveland as well as the Chicago Allerton House. For other clients, they designed the Hotel Governor Clinton near Pennsylvania Station, the residential hotel for women at 18 Gramercy Park, the Fraternity Club Building, and the Barbizon Hotel for Women.

## The Allerton House Chain

The Allerton chain began its association in New York City with the construction, in 1913, of a fifty-room Allerton House located at 302 West Twenty-Second Street in Chelsea. James S. Cushman, a governor of the Society of Mayflower Descendants, named the hotel chain for Mary Allerton, daughter of Isaac Allerton, an early owner of the land on which the first hotel was built. Allerton journeyed to America on the *Mayflower* and eventually settled in the area that is now Greenwich Village.

The company established five Allerton Houses in New York City, initially developed specifically to cater to a male clientele. The second Allerton House was developed in 1915 at 311 Lexington Avenue; it was soon purchased by the YWCA and converted to a women's residence. The subsequent Allerton Houses were located primarily in Midtown on the East Side: 143–147 East Thirty-Ninth Street, 45 East Fifty-Fifth Street, 128 East Fifty-Seventh Street, and the Fraternity Club at 14 East Thirty-Eighth Street. The sixth Allerton House was the exception; 128 East Fifty-Seventh Street was designed as a residence for women with all of the facilities were intended for semipermanent guests.

The chain provided young professionals the services of a hotel and the intimacy of a private club. The Allerton was large enough to provide low rental prices and personal freedoms to their residents, yet it was small enough to encourage community spirit—with none of the religious associations imposed by such organizations as the YMCA or the YWCA, which offered similar residential accommodations. The Allerton was unique. It was not a boarding house, rooming house, apartment building, or hotel; it was a more refined combination. Club hotels were meant to provide housing that was convenient and economical and had greater social cachet than the traditional apartment hotel. They offered many of the facilities and services of the standard apartment hotel, including public dining rooms, housekeeping services, and the rental of rooms on a weekly, monthly, or yearly basis.

Allerton Houses were developed in New York, Cleveland, and Chicago. The Cleveland Allerton Hotel, a 1926 Moorish revival-style building designed by Murgatroyd & Ogden, was later converted to apartments and renamed the Parkview Apartment. The Allerton Hotel in Chicago, also designed by Murgatroyd & Ogden with Fugard and Knapp, was built in 1924. It was Chicago's first high-rise to comply with new zoning laws, and it featured pronounced setbacks and towers. The Allerton helped bolster the redevelopment of North Michigan Avenue into a chic boulevard of exclusive shops, clubs, offices, and hotels.

In a February 1923 interview from *Architecture Magazine*, Architect Arthur Loomis Harmon described the reasoning behind the Allerton House concept:

> The purpose of the Allerton Houses is to give a better grade of living accommodations at a low cost, to raise the standard but not the price. This means the elimination of non-essentials and extravagance in construction. An honest attempt has been made to meet these requirements in the design of these buildings and conform to economic necessities.

Arthur Loomis Harmon was born in Chicago and studied at the Art Institute of Chicago and at Columbia University in New York, graduating in 1901. From 1902 to 1911, he practiced with the well-known firm of McKim, Mead & White, during which time he supervised the construction of the extension to the Metropolitan Museum of Art.

For two years, Harmon worked with the firm of Wallis and Goodwillie, and from 1913 until 1929, he practiced independently. In 1929, Harmon joined the firm of Shreve and Lamb as a partner, at which time the firm's name was changed to Shreve, Lamb, and Harmon. Harmon was active for many years in architectural education and professional societies. He was the president of the New York Chapter of the American Institute of Architects from 1937 to 1939; president of the Architectural League of New York from 1933 to 1935; a fellow of the American Institute of Architects; an academician of the National Academy of Design; and a member of the Century Association, the Bund Deutscher Architekten, the Beaux-Arts Institute of Design, and the New York Building Congress. He also served on a number of juries, among them the national jury for the Reynolds Metal Company annual award for outstanding examples of aluminum structures, and he was on the organizing committee of the Contemporary American Industrial Design exhibit at the Metropolitan Museum of Art in 1940 along with Ely Jacques Kahn.

Arthur Loomis Harmon also was the architectural consultant for the design and construction of Parkchester, Stuyvesant Town, Peter Cooper Village, and the Vladeck City Houses. Harmon's individual works include the Godfrey building at 729 Seventh

# Arthur Loomis Harmon

Avenue (1915); the fourth Allerton House, 551 Madison Avenue (1919); 128 East Fifty-Seventh Street (1921); the Julliard School of Music (later the Manhattan School of Music), 120 Claremont Avenue (1930–34 addition); the Seamen's YMCA (now the McBurney YMCA), 215 West Twenty-Third Street, (1902); 971 Madison Avenue (1927); and 37 West Seventy-Second Street (in association with Donald Hart) (1929).

Harmon's best known individual work is the former Shelton Hotel, currently the New York Marriott East Side at 525 Lexington Avenue. The Shelton Hotel was built in 1923 for James T. Lee. The Shelton Hotel received awards from the Architectural League of New York and the American Institute of Architects. At the time of its construction, the Shelton was considered the tallest hotel in the world, at twenty-four stories. It was praised by architectural historians and critics for Harmon's intelligent treatment of New York's 1916 setback requirements law.

When Harmon joined the firm of Shreve and Lamb, it was already actively engaged in the design of the Empire State Building. Although he took part in the design work, Harmon reportedly never considered the building to be his own.

Shreve, Lamb, and Harmon worked principally on commercial office buildings, although they also designed a number of estates and residences in the New York suburbs and a few apartment houses in Manhattan (such as 130 East Fifty-Seventh Street and 30 East Seventy-Sixth Street, located within the Upper East Side Historic District). Their other buildings in New York included the office building at 500 Fifth Avenue, a 1931 addition to 14 Wall Street (a designated New York City Landmark), an addition to the New York Times Annex on West Forty-Third Street, the Lefcourt

National Building, and the Mutual of New York Building. Outside of New York City, their work included the Standard Oil Building in Albany; the Reynolds Tobacco Company building in Winston-Salem, North Carolina; and the Chimes Building in Syracuse, New York. These tended to be similar to their New York City work, with unadorned limestone cladding, metal-framed windows, and simple, set-back massing, occasionally with Art Deco or streamlined ornamental motifs. Although the firm of Shreve, Lamb, and Harmon designed many buildings, it will mostly be remembered for the design of the Empire State Building.

He died in 1958 in White Plains, New York, at the age of eighty.

## The Design of the Allerton Thirty-Ninth Street House Building

The Allerton Thirty-Ninth Street House is located in New York on the north side of East Thirty-Ninth Street between Lexington and Third Avenues. Plans for a hotel on the site began to be developed in 1916 by A. Stanley Jones of Brooklyn. During the planning phase of the twelve-story hotel, Jones owned lots 35, 36, and 37. By acquiring lot 34, which increased the total square footage of the site, a taller structure was allowed. Jones worked in concert with the Allerton Company and architect Arthur Loomis Harmon to make plans for a taller fourteen-story structure. Upon completion, the Allerton Thirty-Ninth Street House sat on a seventy-one-by-one hundred-foot lot, was fifteen stories tall, and had a total of four hundred rooms.

The Allerton Thirty-Ninth Street House is the earliest example in New York of the Northern Italian Renaissance style applied to a tall building. The Northern Italian Renaissance style was popular from 1890 until 1930 and is traditionally rectangular in plan. Features include the use of arched windows, balconies, terra-cotta, and square towers. Harmon adapted an H-plan and designed the center core as a tower using the hipped roof characteristic of Northern Italian-style architecture. The style is usually marked by varied brickwork and a raised basement adapted for public spaces: dining, reception, and lounge. The balconettes usually found at this level were raised one level, clad in red terra-cotta, and used as ornament. Full-length arched windows and doorways were symmetrically placed and inset with stone trim. Instead of the traditional cornice, Harmon applied large terra-cotta cartouches and a blind arcade band at the rooftop garden.

Built just before the new zoning laws came into effect, Harmon, knowing that the surrounding streetscape would change over time, had the foresight to leave the upper stories exposed on all four sides, creating light courts. Emphasizing the vertical by recessing the window bays, he also chose this style of architecture for its economy of construction. This style quickly became the trademark style for the Allerton Club Hotel chain.

Constructed primarily of red brick with projecting headers, which ascend to a central hipped roof tower, the open sides of the H-plan building face adjacent structures along Thirty-Ninth Street. The prominent roof garden, emphasized by the three arched openings separated by twin terra-cotta columns forming the crown of the building, is a central feature of the hotel's communal facilities, part of the distinctive style introduced by Harmon. The Northern Italian Renaissance style of architecture fits skillfully into the surrounding streetscape. The building's imaginative and graceful combination of details and monumental red brick surface unite to make it one of the most distinguished structures of its time.

The main entrance is decorated with a stone border pattern of abstracted foliage, surmounted by an eagle surrounded by a wreath with ribbons, designed to pay homage to the United States entry into World War I.

The Allerton is a transitional design combining the pared-down ornamentation of later hotels with the massing of earlier buildings. This building became a seminal building for the hotel type and precursor to the design of the Shelton Hotel, designed by Harmon in 1924. Harmon gives a detailed description of the design of the Allerton in an interview in *American Architect*:

> The building was treated as a tower, adopting a symmetrical plan and providing a nearly uniform wall surface treatment on all four sides. Common red brick was used on the front, with a restricted use of terra-cotta trimmings. The main façade of the brick shaft on the streets rises directly from a low granite base. Stone was used to trim the openings of the first floor. On the street façade the brick has been laid up with projecting headers to accent the slight vertical lines of the shaft and with wide and irregular joints, in a subtle attempt to give character to the materials. The appearance of height has been fostered by the accenting of the vertical lines and the elimination of all horizontal ones. Particular attention was paid to the roof garden; this is enclosed by arcade columns forming like a crown on the building, giving interesting glimpses of the East River and the city.

The Allerton Thirty-Ninth Street House was noted for the quality of design and the amenities provided. Public facilities included one or more dining rooms, a reception room for visitors, a library, and a solarium off the roof terrace. The athletic facilities consisted of a swimming pool and a gymnasium that were reserved for residents. All amenities were designed to evoke the exclusivity of club life.

## The Barbizon Hotel for Women

The Barbizon Hotel for Women was built in 1927 as a residential hotel and clubhouse for single women who came to New York for professional opportunities. Designed by the prominent hotel architects Murgatroyd & Ogden, the twenty-three-story Barbizon Hotel is an excellent example of the 1920s apartment hotel and is notable for its design quality. The Barbizon's design reflects the influence of architect Arthur Loomis Harmon's Shelton Hotel in New York. Harmon, who would help design the Empire State Building a few years later, made visionary use of the city's 1916 zoning law to admit light and air to the streets below.

In the period following World War I, the number of women attending college began to approach that of men for the first time. Unlike the graduates of preceding generation, three-quarters of whom had intended to become teachers, these women planned on careers in business, the social sciences, or the professions. Nearly every female student expected to find a job upon graduation in a major city.

The demand for inexpensive housing for single women led to the construction of several large residential hotels in Manhattan. Of these, the Barbizon Hotel for Women, which was equipped with special studio, rehearsal, and concert spaces to attract women pursuing careers became the most renowned. Many of its residents became prominent professional women including Sylvia Plath, who wrote about her residence at the Barbizon in the novel *The Bell Jar.*

The Barbizon's first floor was equipped with a theater, stage, and pipe organ with a seating capacity of three hundred. The upper floors of the tower contained studios for painters, sculptors, musicians, and drama students. The hotel also included a gymnasium, swimming pool, coffee shop, library, lecture rooms, an auditorium, a solarium, and a large roof garden on the eighteenth floor.

On the Lexington Avenue side of the building, there were shops including a dry cleaner, hairdresser, pharmacy, millinery shop, and bookstore. The hotel also leased meeting and exhibition space to the Arts Council of New York and meeting rooms to the Wellesley, Cornell, and Mount Holyoke Women's Clubs.

In 1923, *Rider's New York City Guide* listed only three other hotels catering to businesswomen: the Martha Washington at 29 East Twenty-Ninth Street, the Rutledge Hotel for Women at 161 Lexington Avenue, and the Allerton House for Women at Fifty-Seventh Street and Lexington Avenue.

The Barbizon Hotel advertised that it was a cultural and social center that included concerts on radio station WOR, dramatic performances by the Barbizon Players, the Irish Theater with actors from the Abbey Theater, art exhibits, and lectures by the Barbizon Book and Pen Club.

This rich cultural program, the special studio and rehearsal rooms, reasonable prices, and complimentary breakfasts attracted many women pursuing careers in the arts. Notable residents included the actress Aline McDermott while she was appearing on Broadway in the *Children's Hour*, Jennifer Jones, Gene Tierney, Eudora Weltz, and *Titanic* survivor Margaret Tobin Brown, star of the *Unsinkable Molly Brown* who passed away during her stay at the Barbizon in 1932. During the 1940s, several other performers resided at the Barbizon, including comedian Peggy Cass, musical comedy star Elaine Stritch, actress Chloris Leachman, future first lady Nancy Davis (Reagan), and actress Grace Kelly.

The Barbizon Hotel has been the location of the following popular cultural performances:

- In the critically acclaimed television series *Mad Men*, the Barbizon is noted as the place of residence of one of Don Draper's post-divorce love interests, Bethany Van Nuys.
- In the 1967 Nick Carter spy novel *The Red Guard*, Carter books his teenage goddaughter into the Barbizon.
- In the 2015 Marvel TV Series *Agent Carter*, Peggy Carter lives in the Griffith, a fictional hotel heavily inspired by the Barbizon and located on Sixty-Third Street and Lexington Avenue.
- In Sylvia Plath's novel, *The Bell Jar*, the Barbizon is prominently featured under the name "The Amazon." The novel's protagonist, Esther Greenwood, lives there during a summer internship at a fashion magazine. This event is based on Plath's real-life internship at the magazine *Mademoiselle* in 1953.
- In Fiona Davis's debut novel, *The Dollhouse*, the Barbizon Hotel is featured in a fictitious coming-of-age story that details two generations of young women whose lives intersect.
- Michael Callahan's debut novel *Searching for Grace Kelly*, is set in 1955 at the Barbizon. The novel was inspired by

Callahan's 2010 article about the Barbizon in *Vanity Fair*, titled "Sorority on E. 63rd St."

By the mid 1970s, the Barbizon was beginning to show its age, was half filled, and was losing money. A floor-by-floor renovation was begun, and in February 1981, the hotel began accepting male guests. The tower studios were converted to expensive apartments with long leases in 1982. In 1983, the hotel was acquired by KLM Airlines, and its name was changed to the Golden Tulip Barbizon Hotel. In 1988, the ownership passed to a group led by Ian Schrager and Steve Rubell, who planned to market it as an urban spa. In 2001, the hotel was acquired by the Barbizon Hotel Associates, an affiliate of BPG Properties, which operated it as part of its Melrose Hotel chain. In 2005, BPG converted the building into condominium apartments and renamed it the Barbizon 63. The building includes a large indoor pool, which is part of the Equinox Fitness Club.

The NYC Landmarks Preservation Commission added the building to its roster in 2012, noting that the structure is "an excellent representative of the 1920s apartment hotel building and is notable for the high quality of its design."

## The Hotel Governor Clinton

Designed by architects Murgatroyd & Ogden and George B. Post and Sons, the Hotel Governor Clinton opened in 1929. The *New York Times* (July 28, 1929) described it as "thirty-two stories in height, designed in the Italian style ... it will have an underground tunnel giving direct connection with the subway and the Pennsylvania Terminal." The hotel is directly across the street from the Pennsylvania Station.

Architect Robert A. M. Stern describes the Governor Clinton Hotel as follows:

> Located at the southeast corner of Seventh Avenue and Thirty-first Street, the Governor Clinton was designed by Murgatroyd & Ogden working in collaboration with George B. Post. Departing dramatically from the Imperial Classicism of both the neighboring Hotel Pennsylvania and the railroad station itself, the Governor Clinton, like much of Murgatroyd & Ogden's other work, was executed in what T-Square described as the 'Italianesque' style—the twelfth-century North Italian style with Romanesque detail—here convincingly married to an asymmetrical mass crowned by a low tower pierced by round-arched arcades. Inside, the, Italianesque style was extended to the lobby with its flat paneled ceiling, but was abandoned in the restaurant, a Georgian-style room that stretched along the Seventh Avenue façade.

Architect Palmer Harmon Ogden's obituary in the *New York Times* read in part, "Mr. Ogden graduated from Cooper Union in 1906. In addition to working out the design for the World War I Victory Arch in Washington Square, New York, Mr. Clinton also designed the Governor Clinton and the Barbizon Plaza Hotels in that city."

The hotel was named for George Clinton (1739–1812), the first governor of New York (1777–1795 and 1801–1804). In 1967, the name of the hotel was changed to Penn Garden Hotel, and then in 1974, it became Southgate Tower. In 2004, it was changed to

Affinia Manhattan. It was renamed the Stewart Hotel in 2016—with 618 guest rooms and operation by Highgate Development.

## The Barbizon-Plaza Hotel

The thirty-eight-story Art Deco Barbizon-Plaza Hotel opened at 106 Central Park South in 1930 with 1,400 rooms. It was designed in a modern classical style by architect and decorator Laurence Emmons who worked with the architectural firms of Murgatroyd & Ogden and Lloyd Morgan. The building rises from a street-defining mass to a comparatively slender tower crowned by a roof covered with small glass tiles set on their edges in narrow ribs of reinforced concrete. By day, the tiles shimmered in the sunlight; at night, the Barbizon Plaza's all-glass pinnacle transformed the tower into a prism of light to create the illusion of moonlight.

When it opened, the Barbizon Plaza was recognized as the first music-art residence center in the United States. In addition to the 1,400 rooms with baths, the building also contained three separate balls for concerts, musicals, recitals, dances, and dramatic presentations. There were many studios for artists and sculptors, exhibition rooms, clubrooms, and a glass-enclosed roof for indoor and outdoor activities. Art galleries, exhibition salons, and a completely equipped library were also included. The Aeolian Company installed a large pipe organ at the hotel in 1930, which was moved a year later to the nearby American Women's Association Clubhouse.

Donald Trump purchased the Barbizon Plaza Hotel and the adjacent 100 Central Park South from Banque Lambert in 1981 for $65 million. His intention was to replace the two buildings with a new one which would be "one of the finest pieces of real estate in New York." In a February 1985 *New York* magazine article, Tony Schwartz described "how a bunch of rent-controlled and rent-stabilized tenants in an old building … have managed to do what city agencies, courts, colleagues, competitors and the National Football League have never been able to do: successfully stand in the way of something Donald Trump wants."

The article goes on to describe how Trump and his organization, attempting to evict the tenants, harassed them through "lapses in building security and ignored needed repairs." Trump sued to evict the tenants in 1981 and in newspaper advertisements offered to house homeless in vacated units. The tenants hired legal counsel and received an injunction against the compliance orders in 1984. Trump countersued, and Judge Whitman Knapp rejected the countersuit, ordering it dismissed with prejudice. Ultimately, Trump dropped the eviction suit, and after a final settlement in 1988, the building was converted to a condominium with fifty-one rent-regulated tenants remaining.

# Chapter 10

## Paul Revere Williams

In the course of his five-decade career, Paul Revere Williams (1894–1980), an African American architect born in Los Angeles on February 18, 1894, overcame prejudice and designed thousands of buildings; served on many municipal, state and federal commissions; was active in political and social organizations; and earned the admiration and respect of his peers. In 1957, he was the first African American elected a fellow of the American Institute of Architects. The path he forged has served as an inspiration for young black architects to this day.

Chester S. Williams, Paul's father, died in 1896, when Williams was two years old. His mother died two years later, in 1898, leaving Williams and his brother orphans. When he was six years old, Williams attended the Sentous Avenue Grammar School and said that he was the only African American student in his class.

The 1910 census data lists Paul R. Williams living with Emily P. Clarkson in Los Angeles. She was variously described as Williams's foster mother, godmother, or guardian. In a 1970 interview, Williams described Charles Clarkson as his foster father.

In June 1912, Paul R. Williams graduated with a class of 174 students from Polytechnic High School in Los Angeles, which was described in a June 21, 1912, *Los Angeles Times* article as "the acme of present-day high school educational results."

For the next four years, Williams pursued a self-directed education studying architecture and improving his graphic skills. As a member of the Los Angeles Architectural Club, he participated in the training and competitions offered through the Society of Beaux-Arts Architects (1913–1916), studied architecture at the University of Southern California (1916–1919), and worked as an apprentice in the offices of local architects and landscape designers.

By 1913, Williams worked part-time in the firm of landscape architect/city planner Wilbur D. Cook Jr. where he gained experience in integrating house and garden design plans. Cook's ideas influenced Williams's designs and were evident in the extensive landscaping for the 1926 Baird/Stewart/Garza House.

Cook was known for his landscaping work in Southern California, including the original gardens at the Beverly Hills Hotel, the City Park in Anaheim—now Pearson Park—and Irving Gill's Dodge House. Cook recognized Williams's superior drafting and drawing skills when he assigned him the task of creating the hand-drawn perspective sketches for the park in Anaheim.

After working with Cook, Williams joined Reginald Davis Johnson, a Pasadena architect, from 1914 until 1917. His revival residential designs with patios, loggias, and courtyards created a "true California style" appropriate to the climate and way of life. In a *Los Angeles Times* interview on October 11, 1970, Williams remembered his early career with Johnson:

The first thing he did was put me on a $100,000 home in Santa Barbara. I'd never been in a house that cost more than $10,000. I couldn't guess how a person could spend that much money. I soon found out.

In the March 30 issue of *Los Angeles Builder and Contractor,* Williams is listed as the designer for a two-story commercial building on South Los Angeles Street. Louis M. Blodgett, a successful African American millionaire, was the builder. Paul Williams later built both of Blodgett's homes in 1922 and 1953.

Williams married Della Mae Givens on June 27, 1917, and she supported his career by "providing him with a comfortable setting in which he could visualize, create and turn his ideas into structures." William studied architectural engineering at the University of Southern California from 1916 through 1919 and began working with architect Arthur Kelly, whose design practice specialized in hotels, residences, and public buildings. An example of Kelly's work is the dormitory at Westlake School for Girls in Los Angeles and Playboy Mansion West, Hugh Hefner's Los Angeles residence.

At twenty-five years of age, Williams described his occupation as "draftsman at an architect's office." In 1920, he was appointed to the Los Angeles City Planning Commission and served on the commission until 1928.

The June 1921 issue of *Southwest Builder and Contractor* lists Paul R. Williams's official certification to practice architecture in California. Williams later became a registered architect in the District of Columbia, New York, and Tennessee (AIA Directory 1960).

From 1921 until 1924, Williams worked in John C. Austin's architectural firm. Austin's firm was known for large public and commercial projects. The Shrine Civic Auditorium and Hollywood Masonic Temple (1922) were projects in Austin's firm during the years of Williams's employment. Williams described his position in Austin's office as a draftsman.

Flintridge, named for and developed by Senator Frank Putnam Flint, was a wealthy, segregated suburb near Pasadena. Williams designed scores of homes in this upscale community, including a house for Katherine Flint, the senator's widow. Williams remembered his professional relationship with the Senator: "I got my start doing better homes ... from him (*Los Angeles Times,* October 11, 1970). Eventually, he designed at least ten spec homes in the Flintridge area, and "the development has one of the greatest concentrations of Paul Williams houses" in the region.

Despite warnings that the African American community was not large or wealthy enough to support an architect, Williams found work in that growing segment of society. After acquiring his architectural license, he began to make important connections, including African American businessman Louis M. Blodgett, a Los Angeles entrepreneur with interests in construction, real estate, insurance, and the funeral industry. Blodgett hired the young architect to design a home in 1922 (and another in 1953). In 1924, Williams designed the Second Baptist Church—one of the first major construction projects in the Central Avenue area of Los Angeles.

In 1923, the Community Arts Association of Santa Barbara sponsored one of the earliest small house competitions in the United States. The cost to build the house could not exceed

$5,000. Williams received a "special mention" for his meritorious design. The judges noted his creative placement of a fireplace on the outside terrace. Eight years later, Williams's entry was published in a catalog available nationwide of small house plans.

In 1923, Williams was notified by the executive secretary of the American Institute of Architects of his election to membership. The Southern California Chapter of AIA elected Williams as an associate member on September 30, 1922—a prerequisite for National AIA membership. He was the first known African American member of AIA.

As a young architect, Williams was aware of the injustice he faced for being a black man in a profession dominated by whites, but his tenacity to take on small projects helped him build a reputation. Throughout his career, Williams found it necessary to develop a few "tricks" to impress his clients. Sadly, but necessarily, Williams developed a style of drawing his design sketches upside down because it allowed him to sit across from his white clients, knowing that they preferred not to sit next to him.

In the 1962 AIA Directory, Williams wrote that he opened Paul R. Williams and Associates in the Stock Exchange Building in downtown Los Angeles. He continued working for John C. Austin until he established his own client base.

## Timeline of Architect Paul Revere Williams Projects

## Second Baptist Church, Los Angeles

The Second Baptist Church, the first African American Baptist church in Los Angeles, opened its new facility in Los Angeles's

Central Avenue area. The building was designed by Paul R. Williams and Norman F. Marsh, the official architect of the Southern Baptist Convention. The church pastor insisted that all workmen constructing the church were from African American-owned businesses.

## Twenty-Eighth Street YMCA

Williams's design for the Twenty-Eighth Street YMCA in the Central Avenue area of Los Angeles included Spanish Colonial red clay roof tiles, a row of arched windows on the second floor, and a smooth stucco finish. Bas-relief panels with busts of African American heroes, including Booker T. Washington and Frederick Douglass, provided decorative detail in terra-cotta with vines and scrolls.

In 2011, it was decided by the Coalition for Responsible Community Development and Clifford Beers Housing that the building would receive a badly needed renovation from Koning Eizenberg Architecture. The building—rechristened as the Twenty-Eighth Street Apartments—now has forty-nine affordable housing units and a five-story addition behind the original structure. Williams's design was preserved as much as possible, but a few elements were added to honor it, including a figure of Williams himself on the first floor, a nod to the building's original bas-reliefs of notable African Americans on the fourth-floor windows. The renovation has earned several awards for its environmentally friendly design and commitment to preserving the original structure.

## Hollywood YMCA

Williams's firm was hired in 1927 to expand and improve the Hollywood YMCA, which would open in 1928. Similar to the Twenty-Eighth Street YMCA, the building was considered a Spanish Colonial Revival with ceramic and terra-cotta interior decorative details. Williams reconsidered the circulation within the building in order to allow the managers more flexibility while encouraging members to participate in different activities.

In addition to his work on the YMCAs, Williams designed many of his most memorable commercial projects in this decade: Angelus Funeral Home, Music Corporation of America's headquarters, Saks Fifth Avenue, and Sunset Plaza Apartments. He also began a lifelong relationship with Howard University.

## Atkin Residence

Jack P. Atkin moved into his luxurious twelve thousand-square-foot home, designed by Williams, in 1929 on the eve of the Great Depression. Atkin asked the architect to design a castle on a hill that would bring back "memories of his childhood in England." The sixteen-room Tudor Revival-style residence in Pasadena was built of brick with a slate roof. Williams utilized expensive materials, including oak, marble, custom-designed stained and leaded glass, and "In-Vis-O" roller screens for windows—all at Atkin's request.

Atkins rented the property to movie studios for the movies *Topper* (1937) and *The Bells of St. Mary's* (1937). The famous residence was destroyed in a 2005 fire.

The Depression slowed work for many architects, but Williams's office remained busy. By 1934, Williams had completed more than thirty-six residential estates. Many of his clients were important in the movie industry—directors, movie stars, producers, set designers, and even makeup artists—including Otto Preminger, Corrine Griffith, Burt Wheeler, Lon Chaney, Bill (Bojangles) Robinson, Charles Correll, and Jacob Paley.

## The Role of Interior Decorators

In an interview in 1970 with the *Los Angeles Times* Maggy Savoy, Williams discussed his philosophy of design:

> Know when to quit … People don't always know
> what they want. It is the architect's job to help them
> find it, and keep within the bounds of grace.

When starting a project, Williams preferred to employ the ideas of an interior designer early in the process. In his career, Williams worked with many important designers and design companies, including Harriet Shellenberger, Bullocks of Los Angeles, Frank Baden of Webber Spaulding, Dorothy Draper, Edward F. White, Paul Laszlo, and John Luccareni.

## The Los Angeles Community

In 1933, Williams was appointed to the first Los Angeles Housing Commission by Mayor Shaw. He served on this municipal commission until 1941.

Throughout his life, Williams continued to be active in the community. In 1942, he was named to Citizen's School Committee, a group that "has no other purpose than to bring about the election to the Board of Education the best possible timber" (*Los Angeles Times*, April 19, 1942). Later in 1942, Williams, along with forty-three leading architects, opened an advice service at Mary Louise Schmidt's Architects Building-Materials Exhibit to foster a closer relationship between architects, owners, and manufacturers (*Los Angeles Times*, November 6, 1942).

## Architect Hilyard Robinson

In 1935, Williams became an associate member of the firm Hilyard Robinson and Paul R. Williams in Washington, DC, where he was registered or licensed to practice architecture. He also became licensed in New York.

Together, Williams and Robinson collaborated on many large projects, including Langston Terrace and buildings on the Howard University campus.

## *The Key to Your New Home*

Lewis Storrs Jr. illustrated his book *The Key to Your New Home: A Primer of Liveable and Practical Homes* with photographs of the built designs by important California architects. Williams's residences were featured in the book. Storrs believed that "awkward and superficial copies of historical styles of architecture have proved themselves unsatisfactory" in the twentieth century. It was more important to build a house expressing the personality of the owner rather than forcing the owner to adapt to a classical formula or mathematical design. With this approach, a house was developed from the inside out.

## The Hampton Institute

Williams was one of the speakers at the Thirteenth Hampton Builders' Conference Program. The annual conference was cohosted by Hampton Institute and the National Builder's Association, the national organization for African Americans involved in the construction industry and building trades. Williams led an open discussion on "national building problems" (*The New York Age*, February 13, 1937).

## Portrait of Paul Revere Williams

"I Am a Negro," an essay by Williams, was published in the July 1937 issue of *The American Magazine*. The editor described the essay as "the frankest, most human discussion of the color problem we have ever read."

## AIA Award of Merit for the Music Corporation of America Building

Williams's practice expanded to include commercial buildings with a residential feel. The MCA building was an example of Williams's most famous commercial buildings. The building was featured on the cover of the October 1938 issue of *California Arts and Architecture*. Williams received an award of merit from the Southern California (Los Angeles) Chapter of AIA (American Institute of Architecture) for the Music Corporation of America building.

# The Hotel Nutibara in Colombia

I've been talking with Paul Williams, the Negro architect and he told me about Colombia, a country which is on the uptake ... Mr. Williams actually has been there ... the new thing about Colombia is that it is building a big city hotel, office buildings, clubs, homes ... all along the most advanced style ... A commission was sent to the States to study the hotel architecture ... When the commission reached Los Angeles, it was so enchanted ... it decided right then and there ... that this was the spirit it wanted. Mr. Williams got the job ... The selection of Mr. Williams to do the job was a nice compliment to Los Angeles. (*Los Angeles Times,* April 14, 1941)

# The Los Angeles Home Show

"California Architecture" is the theme of the 1941 Los Angeles Home Show. Air, sunlight and space are important elements used to define this developing style. Photographs, sketches and models by architects Richard Neutra, R.M. Schindler, Cliff May, John Lautner, Lloyd Wright and Paul Williams are among those whose work best illustrates "California Architecture." (*Los Angeles Times,* January 19, 1941)

## Lincoln University Honor

Paul Williams, celebrated Los Angeles, Calif. Architect, received the honorary degree of Doctor of Science at Lincoln University, Mo., June 10, 1941. (*The Crisis,* July 1941)

## World War II

Fort Huachuca, an early nineteenth-century frontier cavalry post near the Mexican border, is home of the famed Tenth Calvary ("Buffalo Soldiers"). These soldiers were members of one of the army's elite African American divisions. During World War II, many other African American servicemen trained at the fort.

In 1942, Williams designed 125 housing units for the army at Fort Huachuca, part of an intensive, eighteen-month building program. An African American company hired Williams in 1943 to design an amusement center for the soldiers in nearby Fry, Arizona. Because of the center's domed oval roof, the restaurant/bar was popularly known to the soldiers as the Greentop. The building included a 6,400-square-foot dance floor, and the bar was decorated with a series of seven original murals by Chicago artist William E. Scott with the theme "New Peace with Victory." An adjacent fifty-room dormitory was designed for married officers and their wives. While hard liquor was not served at the Greentop, it was reported that the soldiers drank more than two train carloads of draft beer monthly.

*The Chicago Bee*, a popular African American newspaper of the time, sent a writer to Arizona to report firsthand on Williams's work at Fort Huachuca. He described the Greentop complex as "the finest Army Recreational Center in the United States" (March 28, 1943).

## Roosevelt Naval Base Project

Between 1940 and 1943, Williams, a member of the Allied Architects cooperative, worked on an important West Coast military project. Begun before the start of World War II, the naval facility was a center for Pacific Theater activities.

*The Negro Yearbook 1941–1946* described a number of Williams's wartime projects for the United States Navy. Building on his successful experience designing affordable, prefabricated metal housing during the 1930s, he formed the Standard Demountable Homes Company of California. This company specialized in the design and construction of temporary, transportable dwellings. His company negotiated with the War Department to develop and build homes for war workers.

## Publications

When World War II ended, seventeen million service personnel returned to civilian life and needed affordable housing. Williams addressed this problem in two pattern books: *The Small Home of Tomorrow* (1945) and *New Homes for Today* (1946). The plans and lifestyles shown in these books reflected Williams's belief in the importance of homeownership and the future of American middle-class housing. Reviews appeared in the important professional journals and design magazines of the day. Architects, builders, and the general public were encouraged to read them and be mindful of Williams's advice.

Paul Williams formulated his small house philosophy throughout his career. The early architectural competitions he entered often centered on designing small, affordable housing using specific building materials. He showed progress with each submission as he imagined what the homes could be. Before he was known as the designer of impressive historic revival homes, Williams was acknowledged by his peers as a master of the small house.

In an essay published in *Ebony* (August 1963) Williams looked back on his career:

> If I were young today I would start with the need for the development of the small home with the thought that a charming inexpensive home could be produced for the masses by forgetting the formula of houses today and mixing imagination with my thinking. What the world needs today is a new concept for a substantial, economical house.

## The Ideal Home

Williams's ideas about the ideal home were included in a lecture series sponsored by the Women's Architectural League. The March issue of *Architect and Engineer* summarizes his views:

> Interior design as well as exterior appeal, color harmony, rendering, and prompt attention to desires to those contemplating the building of a home … are an important part of today's architectural considerations.

## Tennis Club, Palm Springs

The 1947 Palm Springs Tennis Club additions were a joint design project of Paul R. Williams and A. Quincy Jones. From 1939 until 1940, Jones worked as an architect in Williams's firm, but by the time of the club redesign, they were collaborating as equals. Their vision transformed the existing club—with its traditional tennis courts, swimming pool, and dining room—into a complex that fit naturally into the desert environment.

## California State Redevelopment Agency

Governor Earl Warren recognized Williams's character and integrity by appointing him to the California State Redevelopment Agency.

## *Mr. Blanding Builds His Dream House*

In the 1948 RKO movie *Mr. Blanding Builds His Dream House*, Mr. Blanding experienced building a home working with an architect, lawyers, builders, and workmen. It was the first time in film history that a real house was made for a movie set:

> Those who have shuddered slightly at the prospect of what Hollywood will do with *Mr. Blanding Builds His Dream House* may comfort themselves in the news that the Southern California Chapter, AIA, is on the job. Its president has appointed Robert Alexander, Welton Becket and Paul Williams to serve as a special committee to work with William Pereira—also AIA—in trying to make the film a fair representation of architect-client relationships.

*(Journal of the American Institute of Architects,* September 1947)

How to Build a Home for $5,000

> Start small ... Build a small house now, one that is complete and attractive unit in itself, but has a floor plan designed to take more rooms as needed or as your budget increases ... But be sure your plan will give you a pleasing house inside and out ...

> Williams predicts that the "old-fashioned" living room will disappear in modern American homes. Living rooms will become "informal recreation and leisure rooms that open on a backyard garden." (*Ebony,* March 1949)

## Golden State Mutual Life Insurance Company Headquarters

The new Golden State Mutual Life Insurance headquarters was officially dedicated in a weeklong celebration in August 1949. More than ten thousand people toured the building, including corporate officers, California Governor Knight, State Insurance Commissioner Downey, and Paul Williams.

## Ultra-Modern Home Furnishing Store

The March 1951 issue of *Architect and Engineer* described Paul Williams's design for the new Beverly Hills branch of the W. J. Sloane store. The magazine described the five-story building on Wilshire Boulevard as having "many merchandising and display facilities that are unique in the home furnishing field." His design work for the store started in 1948 and was completed in 1951. It included window displays that could be positioned into place by elevators, underground parking for 150 cars, and a model home built within the store "that will feature the latest in correlated groupings of all types of furnishings."

The store was built by Del E. Webb Construction Company and was an example of their collaborative work with Paul R. Williams.

## Community Honors

Williams, along with two others, was honored at a banquet sponsored by the National Conference of Christians and Jews. He was recognized for his efforts to promote brotherhood in the Los Angeles community:

> Williams, an internationally known architect, is a member of the board of directors of 14 organizations and corporations and is known for his interests in the YMCA and the Boy Scouts of America. (*Los Angeles Times*, December 12, 1951)

## Lafayette Square

Williams designed and built a home for his family in the upper-middle-class Lafayette Square neighborhood of Los Angeles. Lafayette Square was home to many influential people in Los Angeles, and by midcentury, it was open to affluent African American professionals. Williams lived in the home until his death in 1980. This house was designated a historic and cultural landmark in Los Angeles County.

## Honorary Degree from Howard University

Williams's relationship with Howard University began in 1931 when he was invited to participate in a campus exhibition highlighting the work of licensed, practicing African American architects. In 1952, he was awarded an honorary Doctorate of Architecture for his professional stature and service to the university. Williams served as a trustee of Howard University from 1957 through 1966.

## Spingarn Medal

The National Association for the Advancement of Colored People (NAACP) annually awarded the gold Spingarn Medal to the African American who performed at the highest and noblest level the previous year or years. Named in the memory of NAACP Chairman J. E. Spingarn, the award called attention to outstanding, high-achieving African Americans and rewarded their achievements.

In 1953, Paul R. Williams was selected as the thirty-eighth recipient of the Spingarn Medal:

> Endowed with creative talent and possessed of a will to achieve success in our competitive system, Paul R. Williams overcame early handicaps of poverty and racial discrimination to win national honor as one of America's outstanding architects.

While accepting the medal, Williams urged African Americans to become active, progressive citizens by becoming homeowners. In his speech, the architect articulated his personal philosophy of achievement. Through homeownership, African Americans could improve their "standard of citizenship and become active participants in American progress and not apart from it."

## This Is Your Life

*This Is Your Life* was an early version of reality television. Emcee Ralph Edwards greeted an unsuspecting celebrity or outstanding citizen at the NBC Television Studios, retelling the story of their life to a curious American audience in less than thirty minutes. The program was famous for emotions and tears and depicted the "famous" as real people.

In 1953, Edwards surprised Mrs. Jesse L. Vann, a newspaper publisher, with the story of her life. Mrs. Vann was one of the few African Americans featured on the show. Her friends Della and Paul Williams provided the pretext to bring her to the studio for the tribute.

## Hollywood Knickerbocker Hotel Renovation

A sketch of Williams's renovation for the Knickerbocker was featured in the *Los Angeles Times* on March 14, 1954. The newspaper described the new front and forecourt in the sketch as a "strikingly attractive design."

## Hospital Projects

Before the development of a vaccine, polio epidemics were frequent in the United States. In 1955, the Communicable Diseases (CD) Building for the Los Angeles County General Hospital system opened with facilities for 256 patients and five hundred to six hundred doctors, nurses, and other specialists. The facility specialized in the treatment of polio. Adrian Wilson and Paul R. Williams were the architects for the CD Building and a related respiratory center at Rancho Los Amigos.

Williams designed many hospitals throughout his career in joint ventures with other architects and solo:

- Los Angeles General Hospital, a complex of five buildings, 1947–1959
- Westview Hospital, Los Angeles, California, 1947
- Tubercular Hospital, Ecuador, 1948
- Rancho Los Amigos Respiratory Center, Downey, California, 1953
- San Gabriel Hospital, Victorville, California, 1958
- Harbor General Hospital, Sacramento, California, 1959
- St. Jude Children's Hospital, Memphis, Tennessee, 1962
- Good Samaritan Hospital (garage) of Santa Clara, 1967

## Service Awards

*Wisdom Magazine* selected important Americans to receive an award for "contributions to knowledge and distinguished service to mankind." On the cover of its first issue in 1956, the magazine featured Albert Einstein. Williams was among the distinguished recipients of the magazine's first award.

Other honorees that evening included Bernard Baruch, advisor to presidents and international financier; Eddie Cantor, comedian; Dr. Will Durant, historian and intellectual; Conrad Hilton, hotelier; Richard Neutra, architect; Pearl S. Buck, Nobel prize-winning novelist; Maxwell Anderson, playwright; and Richard Rodgers and Oscar Hammerstein, Broadway team.

## Tuskegee Institute

In celebration of the Diamond Jubilee Celebration at Tuskegee Institute, Williams was honored with an honorary degree (doctor of fine arts). In a 1957 letter from the Tuskegee Institute's president, L. H. Foster, Williams was described as "one of the persons in America who is doing outstanding work and who is measuring up fully to the highest traditions of their professions."

## College of Fellows American Institute of Architects

In an April 2, 1957, letter from the executive secretary of AIA, Williams was offered the honor of fellowship and membership in the College of Fellows "for your notable contribution in Public Service." Excerpts from letters supporting his nomination included:

> Paul's achievements in Architectural design should not go unnoticed. Over the many years that I have been familiar with his work, I have become aware that it is consistently good, often with a personal touch that makes it recognizable without seeing his name. (Graham Latta, Los Angeles architect, July 1957)

> I know him to be exceptionally well qualified as a designer ... as an individual he is tactful, courteous, considerate and honest. The quality of his work follows suit. (Adrian Wilson, Los Angeles architect, January 1957)

> He has been a member of The American Institute of Architects since 1923 and a year or so ago he was

advanced to Fellowship in the Institute and is now a member of the College of Fellows. He is the first Negro to be so honored. The Institute and is now a member of our College of Fellows. He is the first negro to be so honored. (AI executive secretary)

## The Church of Religious Science

Dr. Ernest Holmes, Church of Religious Science founder, selected Paul as the architect for its new round church in Los Angeles. Dr. Holmes suggested that the devil couldn't hide in the corners of a round building.

## Big Brothers of Greater Los Angeles

Williams was a member of the advisory council of the Big Brothers of Greater Los Angeles. In 1961, actor Ronald Reagan—future president of the United States—served with Williams on the advisory council.

## Honors at Testimonial

*The California Eagle* reported that Paul R. Williams was honored as "one of California's distinguished native sons" at a celebratory breakfast attended by more than three hundred people. Meritorious awards were given to him from various city and county officials as well as the Young Republicans Unlimited for his service to the region. Professor Charles A. Bigger dedicated a poem to the honoree, which was titled "The Man Wanted."

## St. Jude Research Hospital

St. Jude Research Hospital in Memphis, Tennessee, officially opened on February 4, 1962. Williams supported the mission of the hospital and donated the plans to help entertainer Danny Thomas. Thomas spent more than a decade raising money to build the shrine to St. Jude.

## Hundred Richest African Americans

*Ebony Magazine* consulted many experts to create a published list of the hundred wealthiest African Americans in 1962. Paul Williams was included on the list. The magazine stressed that these individuals were "the genuine articles, however, among the sham and sparkle of the Cadillac-and-Chris-Craft set ... honest-to-goodness millionaires often shun the public-eye."

## If I Were Young Today

The essay "If I Were Young Today" appeared in *Ebony* in August 1963 in a series about successful African Americans reflecting on their careers. During the interview, Williams talked about his career choice: "Architecture is the most fascinating profession in the world and one which I thoroughly enjoy." As a young man, Williams knew of only one African American in the profession—Booker T. Washington's son-in-law, William S. Pittman—when he decided to become an architect.

When Williams was deciding on his career path, the profession was exclusively white and male. African Americans were typically trained in the skilled building trades. In an 1899 photograph, students were learning bricklaying and masonry skills at the Hampton Institute.

## Successful American Negroes

In the issue naming Martin Luther King Jr. as *Time's* "Man of the Year," an eight-page photographic essay listed "some unsung Negro successes in American life."

Paul Revere Williams was included in the list of approximately twenty-five African Americans, including:

- Alonzo Wright, Realtor
- Hattie Mae White, school board member
- Henry Lewis, musical conductor
- Samuel L. Gravely Jr., US Navy commander
- Carl T. Rowan, diplomat
- John M. Burgess, bishop
- Edward J. Dwight Jr., astronaut candidate

## Festival at Rockford College

The April 1965 issue of *Negro Digest* described a festival organized by Rockford College near Chicago. The festival celebrated "Creativity and The Negro" and included "architectural renderings by Paul Williams, photographs by Gordon Parks and singing by the inimitable Josh White." This small liberal arts college with a new "forward-looking" president in a conservative Midwestern city organized the festival to reflect the evolving societal attitude toward African Americans and their accomplishments.

Jane Addams, awarded the 1931 Nobel Peace Prize, was a Rockford College alum. She was a pioneering social worker and feminist.

## The Fedco Department Store

Williams designed the Fedco Department Store in Pasadena, California, and used modern concrete technology (shrinkage-compensated concrete). The building was designed with "tilt-up" panels made of expensive concrete—a material resistant to drying-shrinkage cracking and leaking:

> The success of such projects is beginning to point the way to a new era of concrete technology when design need not take into account the phenomenon of drying-shrinkage cracking. (*AIA Journal* October 1966)

## The Dean of Architects

A profile of Paul Williams was published in the September issue of *Designers West*. In the article, Williams described the ongoing challenges of designing California homes. Creating plans for difficult building sites and understanding the client were important elements for "making a home." Williams believed that imagination was the most important tool an architect could employ in solving design problems: "There is no end of things you can do with a home if you use a little imagination."

## Jay Paley House

In 1968, hotel executive Barron Hilton purchased the residence Williams had originally designed for Jay Paley. Searching Beverly Hills for a home large enough for his growing family and lavish entertaining schedule, Hilton selected the classic 1930s residence. An *Architectural Digest* photographic essay highlighted the home's grounds, grand rooms, and traditional elegance. Hilton modernized and refreshed the interior, but he left Williams's design largely intact. Just as Paley enjoyed a good party, the Hiltons noted that "the house has proven to lend itself well to all kinds of social activities."

## Los Angeles Architectural History

Owners of vintage Paul Williams's residences located in historic residential developments showed their appreciation and pride about living in one of his homes by allowing nonprofit organizations to conduct fundraising tours. In November 1969, a classic Williams Spanish Revival mansion in Flintridge was one of five homes the Pasadena Symphony Association included in its annual holiday tour.

To create interest in the fundraiser, *Los Angeles Times* writer Kim Blair interviewed Williams about how he created his personal interpretation of Spanish Revival architecture:

> We were trying to bring back the Spanish feeling to Southern California and for those who wanted something more opulent than the Mission styles we borrowed ideas from the entire Mediterranean area.

Blair noted the rich architectural details still evident in the Williams-designed home, including paneled walls of rare woods, carved cornices, beamed ceilings, custom grillwork, arched windows and doors, and a wonderful flow to the formal public rooms:

> Few artisans today are still doing the elaborate wood carvings, carved masonry and the delicate wrought-iron work which marks the Mediterranean homes built during the '20s.

Though these details were impressive to her modern readers, they were also hallmarks of a classic Williams Spanish Revival design.

The owner, Mrs. A. W. Horton stated, "Even if one could find the craftsmen to do such work, the construction cost would be almost prohibitive" (*Los Angeles Times*, November 16, 1969).

## Fifty Years of Home Design

Nearing his retirement from active practice, Paul R. Williams was recognized by influential Los Angeles interior designers for his mastery of California elegance. A 1934 estate from his "bygone days" was selected as the 1970 Design House West. The decorators refreshed the interior of the thirty-room Barrick mansion on Ambazac Way and brought it back to "modern-day life." Public tours of the house raised money for various cancer-related charities.

To publicize the event, *Los Angeles Times* writer Maggie Savoy interviewed Williams. In the lengthy article, the architect reminisced about his work with famous and powerful clients and the importance of their individual psychologies in personalizing the designs:

> People don't always know what they want. It is the architect's job to help them find it, and keep within the bounds of grace.

Williams's tact, refined taste, and ability to design a home—no matter the size—became his signature. The interview with Savoy was an excellent summary of his aesthetic and work philosophy.

## USC Honors Williams

As Paul R. Williams began to think about retiring from active practice, he was honored by his peers and others in the community. Tributes were announced at a testimonial dinner for Williams. The University of Southern California named a room in his honor in the soon-to-be-completed Watt Hall in the architectural complex. In addition, the creation of the USP Paul Williams Scholarship in architecture was announced. Broadway Federal Savings and Loan Association donated the first check.

## Death

In January 1980, Paul Revere Williams died in a Los Angeles hospital at the age of eighty-five. He was survived by his wife Della, his daughters, and his grandchildren. Though he retired in 1973 from the day-to-day activities of architecture, his firm continued for a number of years (*Jet*, February 14, 1980).

## Seven Outstanding Architectural Projects

### Beverly Hills Hotel, Beverly Hills, California

In the 1940s, the owners of the Beverly Hills Hotel hired Williams to renovate and update the property that catered to Hollywood's stars. With an eye toward elegance, Williams transformed the already famous hotel into an iconic destination. He designed the pink, green, and white color scheme that the hotel is now known for, as well as the script logo that welcomes visitors to its lush grounds. The 1949 renovation—which has remained largely untouched—included the Palm Court Terrace and the Fountain Coffee Room, which was famed for its classic banana wallpaper created by CW

Stockwell. For decades, Hollywood's royalty frequented the hotel because of its impeccable design and understated elegance, which were testaments to Williams's legendary style.

## Founder's Church of Religious Science, Los Angeles, California

They say it pays to have friends in high places. When Dr. Ernest Holmes decided to create a church building to house his congregants, he called on his friend Paul Williams to design the campus. Williams designed an elliptically shaped church building that he felt was "the perfect symbol for the wholeness, unity, unending and all-inclusive power of love" outlined in the Science of Mind teachings. The church sat within a verdant garden peppered with sculptures celebrating renowned philosophers. The entire project cost $3.5 million, and it remained untouched until a 2016 renovation. Today, the church is listed in the National Register of Historic Places.

## Hotel Granada, Bogotá, Columbia

Williams's illustrious career and global reputation prompted the owners of the Hotel Granada in Bogotá, Colombia, to commission the architect to add on to a popular luxury hotel in the 1940s. Williams was tasked with adding a fourteen-story addition to the 1920s building. He added a "bit of California glitz and glamour with a decided South American flair," which produced a commanding complex that covered an entire city block. Several apartment buildings, two nightclubs, twenty shops, and 310 guest rooms resided in the newly renovated space. On April 9, 1948, however, the hotel was badly damaged during the *Bogotazo* riots that followed the assassination of presidential candidate Jorge Eliécer Gaitán. Three years later, the hotel's remaining structures were demolished and replaced with the headquarters of the *Banco de la República*.

## La Concha Motel, The Neon Museum, Las Vegas, Nevada

While Googie-inspired buildings originated in Southern California in the late 1940s, their popularity would expand through the 1960s when Williams was commissioned to design a motel that could compete with the hotel-casinos planted on Las Vegas's famous strip. While Googie architecture is considered "esthetically unrestrained" and at first seemingly incompatible with Williams's style, the talented architect successfully created a drive-up motel replete with neon signs that grabbed the attention of tourists with its bright and bold features while retaining the architect's elegant architectural DNA. Today the 1,100-square-foot La Concha Motel lobby remains, thanks to architectural historians and preservationists; the lobby serves as the visitor's center at the Neon Museum, a museum that features the best (and worst) of Las Vegas's in-your face neon signs.

## Nickerson Gardens Housing Project, Los Angeles, California

Nickerson Gardens, a public housing facility located in Watts, California, opened in 1954. The architectural project showcased Williams's commitment to providing exemplary housing to those who were neither rich nor famous. The 1,100-unit project sat on fifty-five acres and included a neighborhood center, meeting rooms, a gymnasium that could accommodate more than five hundred people, playgrounds, and theater spaces to foster a sense of community among residents. He also provided lush gardens, landscapes, and the strategic positioning of walls within the apartments to instill a sense of privacy within the extensive complex. Williams's approach and aesthetics were lauded as models that future public housing complexes should emulate.

Eventually, however, the well-designed structure created to foster harmony and community couldn't protect its residents from the societal ills that had pushed them there. When the 1965 Watts Riots erupted, Nickerson Gardens was a hotbed, causing government officials to question the wisdom of creating isolated, highly concentrated areas stricken by poverty.

## St. Jude's Children's Research Hospital, Memphis, Tennessee

Before St. Jude's became the internationally known nonprofit that appeals to people's hearts and pocketbooks on TV, the vision for its original design sat in Paul R. Williams's mind. After he designed the home of Danny Thomas, a Tennessee-based entertainer, Thomas invited him to design the one-of-a-kind hospital that would provide research and care for children battling cancer— without any cost to their families. Williams agreed and donated the plans for the first phase of construction. He also served as a board member of the St. Jude's Hospital Foundation. The hospital was dedicated in 1962, and to date, it has served families from every state and around the world. Williams brought to life Thomas's vision for the hospital's groundbreaking work: "No child should die in the dawn of life."

## Sunset Plaza Apartments, Los Angeles, California

In the 1930s, while many Americans dreamed of owning a home, many Angelenos dreamed of living in the city's luxurious apartments in the heart of Hollywood. Designed in 1936 for Hollywood photographer Frank S. Hoover, the Sunset Plaza Apartments offered all of the amenities of a private residence plus the luxurious perks of a hotel: a pool, tennis court, and sprawling landscapes. The apartments quickly became attractive to the city's high-profile residents and became a popular location for studio photo shoots. From 1980 until 1987, the apartments sat on the City of Los Angeles' list of Historic-Cultural Monuments—until they were demolished.

# Chapter 11

## Holabird & Roche

Architects William Holabird (1854–1923) and Martin Roche (1853–1927) made an important impact with their work on early American skyscrapers.

William Holabird was born on September 11, 1854, in Amenia Union, New York, as the son of Samuel Beckley Holabird. Like his father before him, William Holabird joined the West Point Military Academy in 1873 as a cadet. However, after two years, Holabird resigned over a dispute with authorities of the academy and moved to Chicago where he worked as a draftsman for William LeBaron Jenney, an American architect and engineer, who became known as the "father of the skyscraper." While working with Jenney, Holabird gained a strong functional approach to design, which had an emphasis on durability, economy, maximum openness of unencumbered interior space, and generous window area for maximum light and ventilation.

Martin Roche was born on August 1, 1853, in Cleveland, Ohio, and moved to Chicago, Illinois, in 1857. It was there that he attended elementary school and entered the Chicago Art Institute. In 1867, Roche left the Chicago Art Institute and began his career as an apprentice cabinetmaker. In 1871, Roche was hired as an apprentice to Jenney.

In 1880, Holabird started his own architectural firm with Ossian Simonds, which was named Holabird & Simonds. In 1881, Roche joined the firm, and in two years, when Simonds left, the company was renamed Holabird & Roche.

In the beginning, Holabird & Roche saw little success with their business. Work was slow, and to gain company revenue, Roche designed furniture for manufacturers. However, in 1885, business picked up when the firm was commissioned to design its first major building: a two-story shop and apartment block in Chicago. With Holabird's two years of engineering education and planning skills and Roche's artistic talents, the duo would help launch a new style of architecture known as the "Chicago School." They designed skyscrapers and large hotels for cities across the country with a majority of work focused in the Midwest. Of the many buildings they designed in the Chicago area, twenty still stand in its downtown loop.

Beginning with the Tacoma Building (completed in 1889 and demolished in 1929) and the Marquette Building (1895), the firm became well-known for its groundbreaking Chicago School skyscrapers. In addition to this highly successful practice, they also designed large hotels across the country.

## The University Club of Chicago

The University Club's present building, opened in 1908, was designed by architect Martin Roche as the first "gothic skyscraper." It was one of the most important club buildings of its day and

continues to be architecturally significant. According to critic
Franz Schultz:

> There are other historically great interiors in town:
> Auditorium Theater of Adler and Sullivan and Mies
> van der Rohe's Crown Hall are only two of the first
> to come to mind. But among places where people
> convene to enjoy good food and companionship,
> I can think of no single room in this wonderfully
> composed and constructed city that is more
> stunning, that clears the sinuses more speedily
> or whips the viewer more persuasively into social
> attention than Martin Roche's Cathedral Hall.

Other University Club facilities included private dining rooms,
restaurants, squash courts, a pool, fitness facilities, a library, a
business center, an outdoor terrace, an art gallery, and guest rooms.

## Hotel Muehlebach, Kansas City, Missouri

In 1915, the Hotel Muehlebach opened in downtown Kansas City
with twelve floors, five hundred rooms, two restaurants, a tea
room, and a music room. It was the first hotel in the area to have
air-conditioning.

The property, then the site of the First Baptist Church, was
acquired in 1914 by George B. Muehlebach, whose father, George
E. Muehlebach Sr., had founded the Muehlebach Beer Company.
Muehlebach demolished the church and built a twelve-story, 144-
foot brown brick hotel building designed by Holabird & Roche at a
cost of $2 million. It opened as the Hotel Muehlebach in May 1915.

On December 5, 1922, the hotel was the location of the first regular radio program when Carleton Coon and Joe Sanders began broadcasting the performances of their Coon-Sanders Original Nighthawk Orchestra nationwide.

Barney Allis took over the hotel in 1931, and during his lengthy tenure, the hotel welcomed celebrities including Helen Keller, Ernest Hemingway, Babe Ruth, Frank Sinatra, Bob Hope, Elvis Presley, and the Beatles. The hotel also hosted presidents, including Theodore Roosevelt, Woodrow Wilson, Calvin Coolidge, and Herbert Hoover. Missouri-native Harry S. Truman stayed in the hotel's presidential suite so frequently that the Muehlebach became known as "White House West."

In 1952, a seventeen-story western annex, the Muehlebach Tower, was added to the hotel. Allis sold the hotel in the 1960s. The Radisson Hotels chain acquired the hotel in 1976, making it their flagship property at the time. As a result, it underwent a major $6 million renovation, and began operating as the Radisson Muehlebach Hotel before closing a decade later in 1986.

In 1996, Marriott Hotels bought the Muehlebach and made it into an extension of the Kansas City Marriott Downtown, a huge adjacent hotel originally built in 1985 as the Vista International Hotel. They imploded the 1952 Muehlebach Tower annex building, and in 1998, they built a new, modern Muehlebach tower with a similar façade that met current building code standards. A "skybridge" connected both hotel buildings on their second floors. The original 1915 Muehlebach building's lobby and ballrooms were restored and are now used as banquet and convention facilities by the Marriott.

The Barbershop Harmony Society traced its beginnings to a chance meeting in 1938 in the Muehlebach's lobby between two businessmen from Tulsa, Oklahoma. The two found two other men and sang their way through a snowstorm that had marooned all four at the hotel. A few weeks later, they convened several like-minded singers at a meeting in Tulsa, and the twenty-five thousand-member international organization was founded. The two businessmen's original meeting was commemorated on a plaque in the restored original lobby of the hotel.

Among the Muehlebach Hotel's most famous guests:

- During the 1928 Republican National Convention, held across the street at Convention Hall, Herbert Hoover frequented the hotel.
- Howard Hughes had the presidential suite during his 1945 stay.
- The Muehlebach was the White House headquarters for Harry S. Truman during his frequent visits to his home in nearby Independence, Missouri. Truman stayed in Independence but conducted business in the presidential suite in the hotel's penthouse. Truman signed the Truman Doctrine legislation aid for Turkey and Greece at the hotel on May 22, 1947. Truman predicted his upset victory to staffers at the hotel during election night 1948 (although he spent the night out of the media spotlight at the Elms Hotel in Excelsior Springs, Missouri). The presidential suite was later renamed the Harry S. Truman Presidential Suite, following his terms of office.
- Roy O. Disney spent the night in July 1956 before spending the Fourth of July in Marceline, Missouri, with his brother, Walt Disney.

In 1959, the Society of American Registered Architects, founded by architect Wilfred Gregson in 1956 with the mission of "Architect Helping Architect," held its first national conference at the Hotel Muehlebach. Gregson reported to those assembled:

You are the ones who have made the first great step toward a unified profession of architects. You are a living report that will go to every part of these fifty United States.

During the 1976 Republican National Convention, both Gerald Ford and Ronald Reagan made pitches for delegates at the Radisson Muehlebach. Immediately following the 1976 Republican Convention, Robert A. Heinlein was the Guest of Honor at the Thirty-Fourth World Science Fiction Convention held at the Radisson Muehlebach and the Hotel Philips directly across the street. He was booked into the Muehlebach's Harry S. Truman Presidential Suite for the five-day convention held during the 1976 Labor Day weekend.

Among the other celebrity guests who stayed at the Muehlebach were Babe Ruth, the Beatles, and Elvis Presley.

## The Nicollet Hotel, Minneapolis, Minnesota

The original Nicollet House Hotel was built in 1858 by Joseph Nicollet and was demolished in 1923. The new Nicollet Hotel opened in 1924 with 637 rooms to designs by architects Holabird & Roche. One newspaper called it a "Monument to the Civic Spirit of Minneapolis." Its large size and entertainment venues made it a popular option. Its nightclub hosted Glenn Miller, Artie Shaw, Tommy Dorsey, Gene Krupa, and Lawrence Welk, among others.

In the 1930s, the Nicollet was managed by the National Hotel Management Company under the leadership of management pioneer Ralph Hitz with his unique and particular attention to his guests and employees. In the 1950s, a Polynesian-themed bar called the Waikiki Room was added. In 1957, the hotel was bought by the Albert Pick Hotels Company and renamed the Pick-Nicollet Hotel.

During the 1960s, much of the Gateway District was demolished. The Nicollet was saved, but by 1973, the hotel was bought by a church that converted the building into housing. When various proposals for conversion into apartments, office space, or a new hotel did not materialize, the Nicollet was demolished in 1991.

## The Palmer House, Chicago, Illinois

The original Palmer House was built in 1871 by Potter Palmer. He began his career as a bank clerk in upstate New York and later became a dry-goods store owner in Chicago and revolutionized the retail trade. He was the first to make large window displays, to use big advertising spaces to send goods on approval to homes, and to hold bargain sales. He became a brilliant hotel man as he applied his successful department store methods to the operation of his hotel. He saw no reason why clerks, chefs, and headwaiters should not be subject to the same discipline as floorwalkers and counter-jumpers. *The Hotel Gazette* said he could be seen at all hours in the lobby and corridors of the Palmer House watching and directing.

There have been three different Palmer House hotels. The first, known as the Palmer, was built as a wedding gift from Potter Palmer to his bride, Bertha Honorè. It opened on September 26, 1871, but incredibly was destroyed by fire thirteen days later in the Great

Chicago Fire. Palmer quickly rebuilt the Palmer House, which reopened in 1875. It was advertised as "The World's Only Fire Proof Hotel" and contained a grand lobby, ballrooms, elaborate parlors, bridal suites, cafes, and restaurants. The hotel attracted well-to-do permanent residents who enjoyed the spacious quarters, master bedrooms, walk-in closets, multiple bathrooms, housekeeping, and porter services. By 1925, Palmer erected a new twenty-five-story hotel, which was promoted as the largest hotel in the world. The architects were Holabird & Roche who were well-known for their groundbreaking Chicago School of skyscrapers. They also designed the Cook County Courthouse and the Chicago City Hall.

The new Palmer House was once remembered for the fact that 225 silver dollars were embedded in the checkerboard tile floor of the barber shop. They were put there by William S. Eaton, lessee of the shop, who cashed in on the idea within the next few years. Everyone wanted to see that floor out of sheer curiosity—or to verify that an unusual promotion could attract customers.

As one of the longest operating hotels in America, the Palmer House has an outstanding roster of famous guests, including every president since Ulysses S. Grant, numerous world leaders, celebrities, and Chicago's movers and shakers. The Empire Room at the Palmer House became the showplace in Chicago. During the World's Fair of 1933, an unknown ballroom team, Veloz and Yolanda, won the hearts of the city and performed there for more than a year. They were followed by famous entertainers including Guy Lombardo, Ted Lewis, Sophie Tucker, Eddie Duchin, Hildegarde, Carol Channing, Phyllis Diller, Bobby Darin, Jimmy Durante, Lou Rawls, Maurice Chevalier, Liberace, Louis Armstrong, Harry Belafonte, Peggy Lee, Frank Sinatra, Judy Garland, and Ella Fitzgerald, among others.

In 1945, Conrad Hilton went to Chicago to purchase the Stevens Hotel, the largest hotel in the world with three thousand rooms and three thousand baths. After a prolonged negotiation with Stephen A. Healy, millionaire contractor and ex-bricklayer, Hilton acquired the Stevens. Later in that same year, Hilton bought the Palmer House from Potter Palmer for $19,385,000. Hilton hired the recently-discharged US Army Air Force Colonel Joseph Binns who had the ability to manage both hotels. Hilton reported in his *Be My Guest* autobiography: "I had gone to Chicago hoping to buy one gold mine and came home with two."

In 1971, the Palmer House celebrated its hundredth birthday. Octogenarian Conrad Hilton was present for the ceremonies. Chicago Mayor Richard J. Daly said, "Throughout the country and the world, there is no better known nor more highly esteemed hotel institution than the Palmer House … People who have been in and out of our city think of the Palmer House when they think of Chicago."

Chicago's Frankie Laine sang there in '63, bluesman Josh White performed in '66, Tony Bennett sang there in '68, Trini Lopez in '73, and the pop vocal trio "The Lettermen" sang there in '73.

In 2005, the Palmer House was acquired by Thor Equities for $240 million. Joseph A. Sitt, president of Thor, embarked on a $170 million renovation that included upgrading one thousand rooms (out of a total of 1,639), adding an underground parking garage, removing a series of fire escapes that marred the State Street façade, and adding a new bar and restaurant to the hotel's spectacular lobby. Perhaps the Palmer House Hilton promotional literature says it best:

> Situated just blocks from the Magnificent Mile and the downtown Chicago Theater District,

the wedding gift from Potter Palmer continues to delight the weariest of travelers and the most demanding of hosts.

The Palmer House has been a member of Historic Hotels of America since 2007.

## Stevens Hotel, Chicago, Illinois

When the Stevens Hotel opened in 1927, the newspapers wrote of a new Versailles rising on South Michigan Avenue. Designed by architects Holabird & Roche, the building soared twenty-eight stories and occupied an entire city block between Seventh and Eighth Streets. With three thousand guest rooms, it was the biggest hotel in the world. Its brick-and-limestone walls, decorated inside with hand-painted frescoes, contained five restaurants, exclusive shops, and vast ballrooms. There was a bowling alley, a hospital, and a special private room for pets. The Stevens could produce 120 gallons of ice cream per hour. On its roof, you could play miniature golf at the High-Ho Club. "What a grand realization of an ambition and an ideal … is this great caravansary," reported *Hotel World* magazine, "this magnificent palace of hospitality dedicated to Chicago and the world!"

No one had seen anything quite like it before. Yet, just five years after the first two guests—Vice President Charles G. Dawes of the United States and President Gerardo Machado of Cuba—registered, the Stevens Hotel plunged into a disaster no one could have foreseen. The hotel went bankrupt, and the state of Illinois charged its owners with financial corruption. One of them was crippled by a stroke; another committed suicide. In newspapers across the country, the crisis of the Stevens Hotel competed for column inches with Al Capone's imprisonment and Franklin D. Roosevelt's first hundred days in the White House. And when it was over, the Stevens business empire, once one of the most prominent in Illinois, was gone.

Few, if any, of the thousands who pass through the cavernous Chicago Hilton and Towers, as the Stevens is called today, know the dramatic episode of Chicago history that unfolded there. However, it is not just the tale of a gaudy Jazz Age venture laid low by the Depression. The youngest Stevens heir was seven years old when the hotel opened—and barely a teenager as the business crumbled around him—but John Paul Stevens would go on to become a justice of the Supreme Court of the United States.

The Stevens Hotel was in large part the brainchild of Justice Steven's grandfather James W. Stevens. A native of Colchester, Illinois, where he had been a village merchant, "J. W." migrated to Chicago in 1886. A born financier, J. W. made a fortune in insurance and ruled his companies with a firm hand. In due course, he brought his sons, Raymond W. and Ernest J., Justice Steven's father, into his businesses. The LaSalle Hotel was for a time Chicago's largest hotel, and under Ernest's ownership and management, it was also one of its most successful.

But the Stevenses believed that Chicago, the booming hub of the Midwest, needed a state-of-the-art destination for travelers and conventioneers. It needed the biggest hotel in the world. The projected price, more than $28 million, was a fantastic sum in the 1920s—ten times what Yankee Stadium had cost a few years earlier. And so, in 1925, the family launched the Stevens Hotel Company, betting their future on Chicago's.

At first, everything went according to plan. The bonds sold well, having been declared safe by the financial press based on J. W.'s prediction of $2.8 million in after-tax annual revenue. The Stevenses sold their relatives some $350,000 worth of bonds. And why not? Illinois Life itself had bought $3 million worth.

The Stevenses laid the cornerstone at Michigan Avenue and Seventh Street (now Balbo Drive) on March 16, 1926. Buried in a cooper box alongside the massive block was a *Chicago Tribune* editorial praising the venture. At a flag-raising ceremony on the site in May, Ernest passed out cash bonuses to the workers, a token, he told the men, of the "part you played in the construction of the largest and finest hotel in the world."

Ernest planned the building inside and out. Adapting one of the innovations pioneered by the hotelier Ellsworth Statler, Ernest equipped each of the hotel's rooms with its own bathroom—and added a mirror flanked by "two brilliant light globes so that a man can see to shave both sides of his face without guessing," as the *Chicago Daily News* noted. Meanwhile, seven freight cars of glassware for the hotel came from Pennsylvania; ten carloads carrying three hundred thousand pieces of china arrived from a New Jersey factory. The dinner plates bore silhouette images of Ernest's wife, Elizabeth; on the reverse side was Ernest's tribute: "Her silhouette in profile is pleasing to the eye but her own dear self in person makes my home a paradise."

The Great Depression ruined the Stevens family, and the state of Illinois charged the hotel's owners with financial corruption. Like four out of five American hotels during the Great Depression, the Stevens Hotel went bankrupt. The government took the hotel into receivership, and by the late 1930s, it was valued at only $7 million.

In 1942, the US Army purchased the Stevens Hotel for $6 million for use as barracks and classrooms for the Army Air Force during World War II. The Stevens housed men more than ten thousand air cadets during that time, and they utilized the Grand Ballroom as their mess hall. In January 1944, the War Department closed a deal to sell the property for $4.91 million to a bricklayer turned private businessman named Stephen Healy. As World War II drew to a close, Conrad Hilton purchased the hotel from Healy in February 1945. The board of directors changed the name of the hotel, naming it after Conrad Hilton himself, on November 19, 1951. Conrad continued to use his Hollywood connections to entice film stars, politicians, and royalty to the hotel.

Among improvements made to the hotel was the installation of a large ice stage in the Boulevard Room Supper Club, which began featuring elaborate ice shows in 1948. In January 1958, Darlene and Jinx the skating chimpanzee performed. The Hilton Center was added to the building in 1962, featuring a three-level structure containing expanded space, the Continental Ballroom, and the International Ballroom.

In April 1951, crowds gathered in the Great Hall to hear a speech by General Douglas MacArthur defending his conduct of the war in Korea, calling for a new American policy toward the conflict to replace the current "political vacuum."

During the 1968 Democratic National Convention, the streets outside the Conrad Hilton Hotel were the scene of a police riot as antiwar demonstrators, being beaten and arrested, began to chant, "The whole world is watching." Some protestors escaped into the hotel, along with tear gas and stink bombs, and the hotel suffered minor damage as a result of the violence as a couple of street-level windows gave way under the weight of dozens of protesters being pushed up against them by the police.

The Conrad Hilton hotel was aging, and in the 1970s, its demolition was considered. However, in 1984, the hotel closed for over a year for what was then the most expensive hotel renovation ever undertaken, at $185 million. The hotel's three thousand guest rooms were rebuilt into 1,544 larger and more elegant rooms; six hundred were converted to double-sized rooms with two adjoining bathrooms. The reborn hotel glittered and helped sustain a revival period in Chicago's South Loop neighborhood. The newly renamed Chicago Hilton and Towers reopened on October 1, 1985.

In 1998, under a new initiative by Hilton Hotels Corporation, the Hilton name was placed first in branding, and the Chicago Hilton and Towers became simply "Hilton Chicago." Under general manager John G. Wells, the hotel continued its track record of having hosted every US president since it opened in 1927.

The Hilton Chicago is home to the Normandie Lounge, a promenade that was created from panels and furniture from the famed French Line ocean liner, SS *Normandie*.

The Hilton Chicago has been featured in many prominent movies and TV shows including:

- *Empire* (TV series) (2015)
- *Little Fockers* (2010)
- *The Express: The Ernie Davis Story* (2008)
- *Road to Perdition* (2002)
- *Unconditional Love* (2002)
- *Love and Action in Chicago* (1999)

- *US Marshals* (1998)
- *My Best Friend's Wedding* (1997)
- *Primal Fear* (1996)
- *E.R.* (TV series) (1994–2009)
- *The Fugitive* (1993)
- *Home Alone 2: Lost in New York* (1992)
- *The Package* (1989)

The Hilton Chicago has been a member of Historic Hotels of America since 2015.

## The Statler Hotel, Washington, DC

The hotel was built by the Statler Hotel Company and opened on January 18, 1943, in the middle of World War II. Its architect was Holabird & Roche.

When the property opened, travelers marveled at its state-of-the-art features; central air-conditioning, Zeon tube lighting, a copy of *USA Today* delivered each week, and such luxurious accommodations and event spaces were unheard of prior to its construction. The Statler Hotel quickly garnered a reputation of exquisite innovation and became revered by those who experienced its glamour. Since the presidency of Franklin D. Roosevelt, each United States president has made it a point to stay at the hotel and continue decades of unfettered tradition. The hotel has also hosted Princess Elizabeth, Winston Churchill, and Martin Luther King Jr., creating a lasting legacy from notable public figures.

In 1947, Larry Doby, the first black baseball player to integrate the American League, became the hotel's first black guest when the Cleveland Indians were in town to play against the Washington Senators.

Throughout the years, the Statler Hotel has accommodated influential world leaders and been the site for a vast number of historical events. Inaugural balls, private presidential interviews for vice presidential candidates, and presidential visits have all been held at the Capital Hilton. The hotel was the first to construct an official Presidential Holding Room, now known as the Continental Room, for the president to engage in private conversations.

Scenes from the classic 1950 film *Born Yesterday* were filmed outside the hotel and in its lobby, and much of the film is set in one of the hotel's luxury suites, which was reproduced on a soundstage.

The Statler Hotels chain was sold to Hilton Hotels in 1954, and the hotel was renamed the Statler Hilton in 1958. On January 15, 1977, the hotel was renamed the Capital Hilton. CNL Financial Group began co-owning the property with Hilton in 2003. In 2007, the Capital Hilton was among the properties sold by CNL to Ashford Hospitality Trust. In 2013, Ashford Hospitality Trust spun off the Capital Hilton and seven other hotels as a separate company, Ashford Hospitality Prime. In 2018, the parent company was renamed from Ashford Hospitality Prime to Braemar Hotels and Resorts.

- 1943: Notable celebrities Lucille Ball, Fred Astaire, Judy Garland, and Mickey Rooney visited the hotel to support a large-scale war bond drive.
- 1947: The US Conference of Mayors Meeting began to be held annually at the Capital Hilton.

- 1951: General MacArthur crafted the notable "Old Soldiers Never Die" speech in the hotel's elegant Presidential Suite.
- 1951: Princess Elizabeth visited the hotel to attend the Washington Press Corps reception.
- 1959: Fidel Castro spoke at the hotel for the American Society of Newspaper Editors.
- 1965: Following Martin Luther King Jr.'s iconic "I Have a Dream" address, the leaders of the March on Washington returned to the hotel.

The Capital Hilton has been a member of Historic Hotels of America, a division of the National Trust for Historic Preservation, since 2014.

# Chapter 12

## John C. Portman Jr.

John Calvin Portman Jr. (1924–2017) was an American nonconforming architect and real estate developer. He gained a worldwide reputation for designing and developing hotels and office buildings with multistory atriums. He had a strong impact on his hometown of Atlanta with the development of the Peachtree Center complex of hotels and office buildings. The Peachtree Center ultimately included Portman-designed Hyatt, Westin, and Hyatt Hotels, all spectacularly designed and unique.

John C. Portman was born to John C. Portman Sr. and Edna Rochester Portman. He had five sisters. He graduated from the Georgia Institute of Technology in 1950. Portman married Joan Newton. They have six children, Michael Wayne Portman, John Calvin Portman III, Jeffrey Lin Portman, Jae Phillip Portman, Jana Lee Portman Simmons, and Jarel Penn Portman.

When architect John C. Portman Jr. first set up his firm in Atlanta, in 1958, it was in a single three hundred-square-foot room and bankrolled by a hundred-dollar loan. More than six decades later, the firm's employees number in the hundreds—and many of its scores of completed projects are monuments to an era of architectural audacity. The most memorable of these, nearly always enormous and even glitzy buildings, are appreciated by the general public, even while perennially dismissed by the architectural community.

Portman's sprawling portfolio has, until recently, been given scant historical attention. Architecture historians and theorists are beginning to look back on Portman's output and finding much to admire in "Atlanta's architect," as he was sometimes called. Models of his Peachtree Center, the downtown Atlanta district he designed and developed continuously until the 1990s, were exhibited at the Venice Architect Biennale in 2010. And the new book *Portman's America and Other Speculations* (Lars Müller), edited by Mohsen Nostafavi, dean of the Harvard University Graduate School of Design, is an example of this growing interest. Judging by the book's wide range of critical interpretations, his legacy in architecture is gaining recognition.

He may have been a victim of his own success. For Sylvia Lavin, the architecture theorist and curator based in Los Angeles, Portman's professional productivity ran counter to the criteria established by academically minded architecture critics in the second half of the twentieth century:

> The academy had become the place that established the standards for importance. From the 1950s to the 1990s, there was an increasing distinction between success in professional terms and success in disciplinary terms, to the point that it became almost impossible for the two to exist simultaneously.

Portman nevertheless came up against the ire of the American Institute of Architects, which claimed that an architect who was also a developer represented an irresolvable conflict of interest.

From the perspectives of both the profession and the academy, Portman's Janus-faced role made him the exception that proves the rule. "Every moment that Portman succeeded in practice, he lost for favor in the academy," Lavin says.

His professional success was rapid and early, but his first years in practice were not without frustration. Opening his own office immediately after receiving his license, Portman set out without any commissions or leads. His first project, coming just a year later, was a humble one: renovating the local lodge of the Fraternal Order of the Eagles, in Atlanta. Portman, who was a lifelong artist, insisted that a bronze sculpture of an eagle adorn the new street-front façade and was not deterred when additional funds to cover its expense were not forthcoming. He ended up footing the bill himself and donated the eagle as a piece of public art. The experience was one that pushed Portman to take on real estate development as a role parallel to architectural design.

In a 1983 conversation with the architect Peter Eisenman, Portman recalled being discontented as a young architect dependent upon his client's finances and decision-making.

> I came to the conclusion that if I were to have an impact—and not be just part of a process I could not control—I should understand the entire project from conception through completion. That led me to real estate.

In his view, taking on the development side of construction afforded him a degree of artistic independence and a greater measure of control that opened the door to the boldly original design language that would become his hallmark.

In 1961, Portman's foray into real estate development paid off. The Atlanta Merchandise Mart, finished that year, was his first project as both developer and architect. It was also his largest building to date. At the time of its construction, it was the largest structure by floor area in Atlanta. A concrete behemoth, the structure was built around Portman's acute sense of a business opportunity, transforming a downtown office building, which had once been a parking garage, into a wholesale trade hall of a quarter-million square feet. The project, now part of AmericasMart, was a runaway success, and new wings have been added. The office was a small shop when the project was first being drafted led by Portman and his business partner, H. Griffith Edwards, with freelancers assisting with drafting and rendering. One freelancer, then finishing out a one-year stint in the military at nearby Fort McPherson, was a young Frank Gehry.

The 1967 Hyatt Regency Atlanta was the debut of the atrium hotel, the innovation that made Portman famous. Entering the hotel from the street, visitors made their way through a dimly lit tunnel before seeing, all at once, the towering skylit atrium above. The first building of its kind in Atlanta, the hotel created a shocking sense of urban grandeur. Though subsequent renovations have altered the original atrium somewhat, including the removal of the "birdcage" bar, the space remains thrilling. The hotel's commercial success garnered its architect plenty of opportunities to improve on his model in new projects. Soon Portman's name would become synonymous with the atrium.

But the popularity of Portman's buildings did not translate into unanimous critical acclaim. By the end of the 1980s, the Pritzker Prize-winning architect Rem Koolhaas had characterized Portman's atrium as "a container of artificiality" and "a device that spread from Atlanta … to the rest of the world." Even Morris Lapidus, the famous architect remembered for his flamboyant hotel designs, conceded in 1978, "There is just too much going on in some of Portman's interiors." Still, others saw much to applaud. In 1981, the author and journalist Tom Wolfe approvingly referred to Portman's hotel as "Babylonian ziggurats" with "thirty-story atriums and hanging gardens and crystal elevators."

Portman's son, John C. "Jack" Portman III, joined the office in 1973, detailing the design of the Detroit Renaissance Center's revolving restaurant before working on the Bonaventure. Jack, who now runs Portman and Associates, feels that detractors have missed the point of his father's work:

> Many architects design for the architecture critic, who can get them a good review, but the critic isn't necessarily the user of the building. A lot of the work we did early on is massive, but it's all focused on human scale. It's the one thing that is consistent, from the beginning. The basic philosophy is that architecture is an organic creation focused on the needs of the human being.

The firm's recent projects bear few of the aesthetic markers—scale notwithstanding—that dominated the work of its heyday. Though still operating out of Atlanta, the office is completing new buildings around the world.

Grace A. Tan, who joined the office as an intern in 1985 and is now president of the company, sees continuity between the firm's past and its present:

> Our history is what made us who we are, and it's the inspiration for what we do now. Looking back at all the accomplishments of this firm inspires us to continue to strive, and look forward to what we can do next."

Today, it's not unusual for Portman to be celebrated. His architecture, with its vast scale and glittering interiors, offers a radically optimistic vision of the future that resonates deeply in a present time of seemingly unprecedented uncertainty. Jennifer Bonner, an architect and assistant professor of architecture at Harvard, praises Portman's "pizzazz"—what she calls the architect's trademark "flair, zest, and sparkle." For her, Portman is a paragon of tenacity:

> As a Southern architect working in Atlanta, Portman quietly invented a new type, the super atrium, without being part of a larger discourse. Due to his insistence, a kind of brute force as architect-developer, Portman found a way to experiment with architecture on his own terms. Portman's architecture is part of a new and different canon.

For many young architects, Portman's long career represents a high standard of creative gumption. While a previous generation condemned the joining of architecture and development in a single figure, few millennials are unpersuaded by the monumental products of Portman's efforts. The wildly original works of this hybrid architect-developer stand in stark contrast to the often-banal and sometimes-destructive creations of unfettered real estate development that are the tradition of modern city-building in the United States.

Adam Nathaniel Furman, a London-based designer, sees a distinctly American form of determination and beauty at the heart of the work:

> Portman's American vision of beauty is vast, swaggering, vigorous confidence. It is an incredible belief in the future, that everything is going to be better, everything is going to be bigger, and everything is going to be spectacular. I hope that America produces more architects that represent it in the way that Portman did.

## Portman's Portfolio

In chronological order by first-listed completion date; for complexes, by completion date of first building in complex:

An asterisk (*) following a listing indicates a work done in partnership with H. Griffith Edwards.

1960s

- AmericasMart (formerly the Atlanta Market Center), Atlanta
- AmericasMart 1 (also known as the Merchandise Mart), 1961*
- AmericasMart 2 (also known as the Gift Mart), 1992
- AmericasMart 2 West, 2008
- AmericasMart 3 (also known as the Apparel Mart), 1979

- Atlanta Decorative Arts Center (ADAC), Peachtree Hills, Atlanta, 1961
- Cary Reynolds Elementary (formerly Sequoyah Elementary and Northwoods Area Elementary), 1961
- Sequoyah Middle School (formerly Sequoyah High School), 1963
- 230 Peachtree Building (formerly the Peachtree Center Tower), Atlanta, 1965*
- Antoine Graves, Atlanta, 1965*
- Antoine Graves Annex, Atlanta, 1966*
- Henderson High School, Chamblee, 1967*
- Peachtree Center, Atlanta
- Peachtree Center North (formerly the Atlanta Gas Light Tower), 1967*
- Peachtree Center South, 1969
- Peachtree Center International Tower (formerly the Peachtree Cain Building), 1972*
- Harris Tower, 1975*
- Marquis One, 1985
- Marquis Two, 1989
- Hyatt Regency Atlanta (formerly the Regency Hyatt House), 1967*
- Hyatt Regency O'Hare, Rosemont, 1969

1970s

- BlueCross BlueShield of Tennessee (now the Westin Chattanooga Hotel), Chattanooga, 1971
- Embarcadero Center, San Francisco
- One Embarcadero Center, 1974 (formerly the Security Pacific Tower), 1971
- Two Embarcadero Center, 1974

- Three Embarcadero Center (formerly the Levi Strauss Building), 1977
- Four Embarcadero Center, 1982
- Hyatt Regency San Francisco (also known as Five Embarcadero Center), 1973
- Embarcadero West, 1989
- Le Méridien San Francisco (formerly the Park Hyatt San Francisco), 1988
- Hyatt Regency Houston, 1972
- The Mall at Peachtree Center, Atlanta, 1973
- The Tower (formerly the Block 82 Tower, Bank One Tower, Team Bank, Texas American Bank, and Fort Worth National Bank Building), Fort Worth, 1969–1974
- Westin Peachtree Plaza Hotel, Atlanta, 1976
- Westin Bonaventure Hotel, Los Angeles, 1974–1976
- Renaissance Center, Detroit
- Detroit Marriott at the Renaissance Center (formerly the Detroit Plaza Hotel, The Westin Hotel Renaissance Center Detroit), 1973–1977
- Renaissance Center Tower 100, 1973–1977
- Renaissance Center Tower 200, 1973–1977
- Renaissance Center Tower 300, 1973–1977
- Renaissance Center Tower 400, 1973–1977
- Renaissance Center Tower 500, 1979–1981
- Renaissance Center Tower 600, 1979–1981

## 1980s

- The Regent Singapore (formerly the Pavilion InterContinental Hotel), Singapore, 1982
- George W. Woodruff Physical Education Center
- Emory University, 1983

- Peachtree Center Athletic Club, Atlanta, 1985
- Atlanta Marriott Marquis, 1985
- Hyatt Regency Jeju, Jungmun, Jeju-do, South Korea, 1985
- Marina Square, Singapore
- Marina Square Shopping Centre, 1985
- Mandarin Oriental Singapore, 1985
- Marina Mandarin Singapore, 1985
- The Pan Pacific Singapore, 1986
- Cottage 428, Sea Island, 1985
- New York Marriott Marquis, New York City, 1982–1985
- R. Howard Dobbs University Center
- Emory University, 1986 (to be demolished)
- Northpark Town Center, Sandy Springs
- Northpark 400, 1986
- Northpark 500, 1989
- Northpark 600, 1998
- JW Marriott San Francisco Union Square (formerly the Pan Pacific San Francisco and Portman Hotel), 1987
- American Cancer Society Center (formerly the Inforum Technology Center), Atlanta, 1989
- Riverwood 100 (formerly the Barnett Bank Building), Vinings, 1989

## 1990s

- Shanghai Centre, Shanghai, China, 1990
- Shanghai Centre West Apartment (also known as the Exhibition Centre North Apartment 1)
- Shanghai Centre Apartments 2 (also known as the Shanghai East Apartment)
- The Portman Ritz-Carlton, Shanghai (formerly the Shanghai Centre Main Tower and Portman Shangri-La Hotel)

- SunTrust Plaza (formerly One Peachtree Center), Atlanta, 1992
- Cap Square (short for Capital Square), Kuala Lumpur, Malaysia
- Menara Multi Purpose (also known as the Capital Square Tower 1), 1994
- Capital Square Condominiums, 2007

2000s

- Bank of Communications, Shanghai, China, 2000
- Shi Liu Pu Building (also known as the Bank of Telecommunications), Shanghai, China, 2000
- Bund Center, Shanghai, China, 2002
- Bund Center (also known as the Shanghai Golden Beach Tower)
- The Westin Bund Center, Shanghai
- Westin Residences
- Westin Warsaw Hotel, Warsaw, Poland, 2001–2003
- Beijing Yintai Centre (also known as the Silvertie Center), Beijing, China, 2002–2007
- Beijing Yintai Centre Tower 1
- Beijing Yintai Centre Tower 2
- Beijing Yintai Centre Tower 3
- The Westin Charlotte, Charlotte, 2003
- Tomorrow Square (contains the JW Marriott Hotel Shanghai at Tomorrow Square), Shanghai, China, 1997–2003
- Taj Wellington Mews Luxury Residences, Mumbai, India, 2004
- Renaissance Schaumburg Convention Center Hotel, Schaumburg, 2006
- ICON, San Diego, 2004–2007

- Hilton San Diego Bayfront (also known as the Hilton San Diego Convention Center Hotel and Campbell Shipyard Hilton), San Diego, 2006–2008
- CODA Tech Square, Atlanta, Georgia, Georgia Institute of Technology, Midtown Atlanta, 2017

Awards and Honors

- 1978: Medal for Innovations in Hotel Design—American Institute of Architects
- 1980: Silver Medal Award for Innovative Design—American Institute of Architects, Atlanta Chapter
- 1984: Urban Land Institute Award for Excellence—for Embarcadero Center
- 2009: The Lynn S. Beedle Lifetime Achievement Award—Council on Tall Buildings and Urban Habitat
- 2011: The Atlanta City Council renamed Harris Street in Downtown Atlanta as John Portman Boulevard at Historic Harris Street.
- 2013: Four Pillar Award—Council for Quality Growth

Portman died on December 29, 2017, aged ninety-three. He was survived by his wife Jan; his children, Michael, Jack, Jeff and his wife Lisa, Jana and her husband Jed, and Jarel and his wife Traylor; his siblings Glenda Portman Dodrill, Anne Portman Davis, Joy Portman Roberts and her husband Phil; nineteen grandchildren, five great-grandchildren, many nieces, nephews, cousins, and other relatives and loved ones.

# Chapter 13

## Henry Hohauser

The celebrated Art Deco architect Henry Hohauser (1895–1963) was born in New York. He studied architecture at the Pratt Institute in Brooklyn before relocating to Florida in 1932. His work on Miami Beach, even during the Great Depression, included hotels, theaters, stores, apartment buildings, and private houses. He focused on middle-class investors who could afford the work of an architect of Hohauser's caliber and reputation. He designed more than three hundred buildings, many of which are part of the Miami Beach Art Deco Historic District.

Before there was a Las Vegas, there was Henry Hohauser's Miami Beach. The PBS show *American Experience* called Henry Hohauser and L. Murray Dixon the principal architects of Deco South Beach, which included such architectural features as streamlined curves, jutting towers, eyebrow windows, and neon lighting.

Some of Hohauser's historic buildings are still standing:

> Name: Park Central Hotel
> Location: 640 Ocean Drive
> Architect: Henry Hohauser

Year: 1937
Brief Description: Known as "The Blue Jewel" of Ocean Drive, this pastel-hued classic is the famed street's tallest Art Deco hotel, and its grand lobby once welcomed celebrities such as Clark Gable, Carole Lombard, and Rita Hayworth. The Park Central has elaborate decorative motifs: an inset porch, porthole windows above the entrance, echoed by circular motifs at the top, a tripartite front with vertical fluting, abstract designs in the spandrels of the central bay, and a sleek stainless steel sign.

Name: The Colony Hotel
Location: 736 Ocean Drive
Architect: Henry Hohauser
Year: 1935
Brief Description: The Colony Hotel is one of the best known hotels in the street. There are several series of thin horizontal bands on either side of the sign and short vertical bars along the central part of the roofline with a zig-zag pattern on both sides. At night, the character of the whole area changes when the neon is lit.

Name: Edison Hotel
Location: 960 Ocean Drive
Architect: Henry Hohauser
Year: 1935
Brief Description: The Mediterranean-style hotel temporarily served as a training headquarters for World War II soldiers. The urge to recreate medieval

Spain was popularized in the 1920s and persisted into the 1930s. Carrying out this Hispanic theme, Hohauser dressed up the concrete façade with Romanesque motifs, such as the twisted columnettes.

Name: Essex House Hotel
Location: 1001 Collins Avenue
Architect: Henry Hohauser
Year: 1938
Brief Description: The Essex, like the Tiffany, wraps around the corner of the avenue and is prominently announced by a finial that bears its name. This hotel has all the deco elements: porthole windows along the top floor, eyebrows providing shade for the windows on the lower floors, and a rounded corner with the hotel name in neon.

Name: Cardozo Hotel
Location: 1300 Ocean Drive
Architect: Henry Hohauser
Year: 1939
Brief Description: Like the Carlyle Hotel across Thirteenth Street, the Cardozo Hotel is also curvilinear. Although there is a strong sense of horizontality, accented by the bands of eyebrows and modified string courses, both the side and front facades have emphatic central bays as well.

Name: Crescent Hotel
Location: 1420 Ocean Drive
Architect: Henry Hohauser

Year: 1938

Brief Description: Unlike most Art Deco facades, this is asymmetrical, although one can still see it as a three-part façade. Like some Art Deco structures, though, it has relief decoration. It is located just beside another jewel: the McAlpin Hotel.

Other Hohauser Buildings in Miami Beach

- The Novick (1937) 610 Jefferson Avenue
- The Century Hotel (1939) 140 Ocean Drive
- The Edison Hotel (1935) 960 Ocean Drive
- The Davis (1941), formerly the Park Washington Resort, which is actually a collection of four hotels: the Davis, Taft, Belaire and Kenmore.
- Collins Plaza (1936) 318 Twentieth Street, renovated in 2013 and renamed Riviera Suites
- Collins Park Hotel (1939), 2000 Park Avenue. It includes a glass entryway and rounded corners.
- Neron Hotel, (1940) 1110 Drexel Avenue. It was demolished in 1982.
- The Parc Vendome (1936), 736 Thirteenth Street
- 1020 Sixth Street Apartments
- 5363 LaGorce Drive

Henry Hohauser was considered one of the most prolific architects in Florida. When he got his architectural license in New York, he started working for his cousin William Hohauser. When he realized that he was underpaid, he left and started his own business. Henry hired an ex-model as his secretary, and in 1923, he and Grace were married. They remained together until his death in 1963 at age sixty-eight.

Two of Henry Hohauser's most successful projects are still in operation: the Congregation Beth Jacob (1929) and the Greystone Hotel (1939).

Congregation Beth Jacob (founded 1927) was the first Jewish congregation in Miami Beach to erect a synagogue in 1929 at 311 Washington Avenue. As the congregation expanded, a new, larger building was built in 1936 next door, designed by congregation member and noted Art Deco architect Henry Hohauser. The synagogue was Hohauser's first project on Miami Beach.

This structure boasts seventy-seven colorful stained glass windows, eight Art Deco chandeliers, marble bimah, decorative exterior concrete relief panels, and a copper Moorish dome. In its original configuration, the building held 850 people in theater-style seating with a women's balcony. The floor was sloped to allow worshippers to see and hear the religious services.

The newer structure was built in 1936 with the same elements and materials as the adjacent original synagogue that was built seven years earlier. The front elevations of both buildings have the same gable and two-story rectangular plans. The central double door of 301 Washington Avenue has inset panels, highlighting the Star of David. The main entrance is elevated by ten steps surfaced in tile and is approached from three sides. Above the door is a large arched stained glass window that represents the giving of the Ten Commandments to the Jews on Mount Sinai with the rays of the divine presence streaming down from the clouds. The entrance is flanked by coupled fluted pilasters of cast stone, topped by composite capitals with the fluting continuing in the arch. The original light fixtures and stair railings remain. Multicolor Art Deco friezes with the Star of David are located between the first- and second-floor windows on all four sides of the building.

A copper dome mounted in an octagonal drum crowns the outside of the building. Each side of the drum has an octagonal stained glass window with a central Star of David. The rear elevation is a symmetrical composition with windows flanking the central projecting beam. Above, a stained glass window depicts the menorah.

The interior ceiling is a shallow barrel vault with seven Deco chandeliers and another larger chandelier suspended from the top of the copper dome. Six arches in the ceiling connect twelve columns on the northern and southern walls. The columns contain the Star of David and menorah-like sconces.

When the structure was built, it had no air-conditioning. The transparent glass windows had to be opened during services, letting in the street noises and the beach's blowing sand and dust. When Rabbi Moses Mescheloff (spiritual leader from 1937–1955) addressed the congregation with the windows and doors open, he had to speak so loudly that he could be heard a block away. The sun shone so brightly that it was impossible for the worshippers to read their prayer books.

The solution was determined by installing air-conditioning and stained glass windows that were designed by Rabbi Mescheloff with graphic symbols to proclaim the messages of the foundations of Judaism. They create an environment beautifully enriched with the aspirations of the principles of the Jewish faith. The stained glass windows, installed in 1940, were fabricated in Hialeah.

The Greystone Hotel is located in the heart of South Beach, the southern neighborhood of the coastal city of Miami Beach, and dates back to 1939. It was designed by renowned architect Henry

Hohauser, who was given the title of "Great Floridian" by Florida's Department of State in 1993 for his major contribution to the distinct Art Deco architectural scene present throughout the region.

The Greystone Hotel will soon complete a $65 million restoration, bringing a new life to its ninety-one boutique guest rooms. Guests will have several options to enjoy throughout the hotel, from a rooftop poolside lounge with DJs and unique food options to a mixology-driven whiskey lounge. There will also be a speakeasy perfect for those seeking a unique experience to enjoy a cocktail or two.

The Greystone Hotel is the ideal destination for those wishing to experience the best of what South Beach has to offer. Guests who venture a block away from the front doors of the hotel will find the sparkling blue waters of the Atlantic Ocean and seven miles of beautiful beaches throughout Miami Beach. The hotel is situated within walking distance from a selection of attractions to experience: the Philip and Patricia Frost Museum of Science or sloths or lemurs at Jungle Island. The Wynwood Walls offers a unique experience for those interested in visual arts.

In 1970, when Polly Redford wrote the *Billion-Dollar Sandbar: A Biography of Miami Beach,* the so-called Art Deco buildings were not held in high regard:

> In tune with a new, less affluent era, these buildings were no longer, Spanish baroque, for even the cheapest imitation loggias, balconies, tiled roofs and plaster gargoyles used up extra money and space; they followed instead the then "modern" architecture of the day, a style whose angular lines, flat sundecks and staring windows suggested a series of stranded ferry boats parsimoniously cut up and converted into hotels.

Redford's 1970 devaluation of the Art Deco hotels was contradicted by Barbara Capitman, a New York design journalist who came to Miami in 1973. She and a young designer, Leonard Horowitz, initiated a revolution in Miami Beach that has been represented since 1979 by the National Registry of Historic Places designation for 1,200 buildings in Miami Beach.

Veteran Miami journalist Howard Kleinberg wrote in *Woggles and Cheese Holes: The History of Miami Beaches Hotels* (2005):

> The newer architects had no idea that what they were designing eventually would be called Art Deco. Their work at the time carried various descriptions, including Zig Zag, Moderne, Streamline, and Depression Moderne. At the forefront of the new movements were Roy France, Henry Hohauser and L. Murray Dixon. At the time they were built, the hotels were as unnoticed as the men who designed them; or of the men who built them, such as Russian immigrant Irving Miller, who at times owned the Cardoza, Carlyle, Hadden Hall, Claremont and Richmond hotels.

Commissioned by the Greater Miami and the Beaches Hotel Association, the 124-page book recounts the story of Miami Beach's building booms and lean times, the developers who succeeded and failed, and their architects.

The Greystone Hotel has been a member of the Historic Hotels of America since 2018 and is listed on the National Register of Historic Places.

# Chapter 14

## Dorothy Draper

Dorothy Draper (1889–1969) was a famous American interior designer. Stylistically, she used bright, exuberant colors and large prints that would encompass whole walls. She incorporated black and white tiles, rococo scrollwork, and baroque plasterwork, design elements now considered definitive of the Hollywood Regency style of interior decoration.

She was born into the aristocratic Tuckerman family in Tuxedo Park, New York, one of the first gated communities in the United States. Her parents were Paul Tuckerman and Susan Minturn. In addition to the house in Tuxedo Park, the family also had a Manhattan townhouse and a summer cottage in Newport, Rhode Island.

Draper's great-grandfather, Oliver Wolcott, was a signer of the Declaration of Independence. Draper's cousin, Sister Parish, also became a major interior designer of the twentieth century. Educated primarily at home by a governess and tutor, Draper spent two years at the Brearley School in New York City.

Draper married Dr. George Draper in 1912 and redecorated her homes in such style that other high society friends began to do the same for their homes. Her husband was the personal doctor to

President Franklin D. Roosevelt after he was diagnosed with polio. Since Eleanor Roosevelt and Dorothy were cousins and good friends growing up, the relationship between the two families was already in existence. The Drapers had three children, and as they bought and sold houses, Dorothy Draper developed a reputation as having a flair for decorating. Dorothy and George Draper divorced in 1930.

A century ago, the average Upper East Side society matron was not expected to do a great deal more with her day—or her life—than entertain other society matrons, support the odd artist or charity, and raise a few heirs. Dorothy Tuckerman Draper was far from the average Upper East Side society matron. Tall, beautiful, and unflaggingly confident, she set up her own interior design business in 1925, and a decade later, she was on her way to being the most famous decorator, if not the most famous businesswoman, in America. Driven purely by her own idiosyncratic taste—she was famous for the dictum "if it looks right, it is right"—she transformed down-at-heel apartment buildings into the most desirable addresses in town and established the resort hotel as the quintessential 1930s space of leisure. Moreover, she did it all alone—after her husband made off with another woman in the same week as the Wall Street Crash.

That one-two punch did not slow her down for long. During the Depression, Draper honed her signature style at hotels, resorts, restaurants, and nightclubs across the country, transforming them into stylish, slightly surreal stage sets. In New York, she put her stamp on the cafeteria at the Metropolitan Museum of Art, the Coty Salon in Rockefeller Center, and the Carlyle and Hampshire House Hotels; in Chicago, she made over the Camellia House restaurant; and in West Virginia and Southern California, the Greenbrier and Arrowhead Springs resorts were all-inclusive Draper worlds. Her signatures, or "Draperisms," included massive black-and-white checkerboard floors, elaborate plaster moldings and stripes so wide they had to be painted by hand, and her trademark cabbage rose chintz, with its clusters of overblown blooms, sold by the mile.

She hated milquetoast pastels and muddy neutrals; they were the chromatic equivalent of what she called the "will to be dreary," a "morose little imp" that tells us not to spend time or money on things we know would be frivolous and fun. Dorothy Draper's exuberant, saturated color schemes—a riot of chartreuse, crimson, sky blue, and shiny black—were quite the opposite. They were optimism incarnate.

Encouraged by her clients, Draper started Architectural Clearing House in 1925. It was "arguably the first official interior design business." After several successful apartment lobby renovations, Draper changed the firm's name to Dorothy Draper and Company in 1929.

Draper's first big break came in the early 1930s when Douglas Elliman hired her to redecorate the Carlyle Hotel on Madison Avenue in Manhattan. This would be the first of many important hotel commissions. Draper was again hired by Elliman to redecorate a block of former tenement homes (today known as Sutton Place) because prospective buyers were not purchasing the homes. The dirty brick exteriors were painted black, with contrasting white windowsills and doors in primary colors. The dingy hallways were brought to life with flowered carpets and wallpaper. Soon, the apartments that the owners had struggled to rent at fifteen dollars a month were fully occupied at more than sixty dollars a month. Sutton Place became one of the most exclusive neighborhoods in New York. The decorator herself would be a tenant, moving in with her youngest daughter and her dalmatian, sharing a "bandbox" one-bedroom apartment that she painted sky-blue from floor to ceiling.

However, few people wanted to bring in quite as much color as Dorothy Draper. Not wanting to be restricted by a client's cautious taste, she began to pursue spaces that other private decorators weren't interested in, spaces that many people overlooked, spaces that would eventually make her famous: hotels and resorts. It helped that the commercial developers and architects in charge of these spaces were almost always men, generally those she met through her society connections, who were happy to throw up their hands at details like the depth of a closet or the position of a mirror and defer to DD's feminine insights.

In 1928, she took on the lobby of the Carlyle Hotel on Seventy-Sixth street through her friend, the real estate magnate Douglas Elliman, and laid a bold black-and-white marble floor, a look that would become a signature. With oversized mirrors, chandeliers, marble columns, and classical busts, softened with satin and velvet, the small, transient space became a place to enjoy. Even though the hotel went bust in the Great Depression before it had even opened, it was the first step toward her real life's work: reconceiving the public spaces of hotels not as bland pass-throughs but eye-catching meeting and social spaces. The Carlyle Hotel was sold and reopened later in the 1930s, when DD was hired to decorate the whole interior.

Draper created a new style known as "Modern Baroque," adding a modern flair to a classical style. She used dramatic interior color schemes and her trademark cabbage-rose chintz. She promoted shiny black ceilings, acid-green woodwork, and cherry-red floors, believing that "lovely, clear colors have a vital effect on our mental happiness." She also chose very dramatic and contrasting color schemes, such as black with white and adding in bits of color. She combined different colors, fabrics, and patterns together, combining stripes with floral patterns. She often used large, oversized details and numerous mirrors. All of the colors and patterns contributed to her dramatic design were referred to as "the Draper touch." The opposite of minimalism, her designs were incorporated in homes, hotels, restaurants, theaters, and department stores.

By 1937, Draper had become a household name, and her aesthetic enthusiasm was adopted by suburban housewives. F. Schumacher sold more than a million yards of her cabbage-rose chintz in the 1930s and 1940s. The Draper bedroom scheme of wide pink and white wallpaper, chenille bedspreads, and organdy curtains soon became ubiquitous across the country.

Draper did a great deal of hotel design, including the Sherry-Netherland in New York, the Drake in Chicago, and the Fairmont in San Francisco. At the height of the Depression, she spent $10 million designing the Palácio Quitandinha in Petrópolis, Rio de Janeiro.

In 1937, Draper created a top-to-bottom decorative scheme for New York's exclusive Hampshire House apartment hotel, giving the lobby a bold black-and-white checkerboard floor, a thick glass Art Deco mantelpiece surround, Victorian-style wing chairs, and neo-Baroque plaster decorations. She found artisans in Brooklyn who could fashion enormous scroll-and-shell bas reliefs, floral swags, and multi-arm chandeliers. Her use of sliding glass doors rather than shower curtains at Hampshire House was considered innovative.

During the Great Depression, the "Ask Dorothy Draper" column ran in seventy newspapers. She advised people to "take that red and paint your front door with it," and many people followed her advice. They also bought more than a million yards of her signature cabbage rose fabric.

One of Dorothy Draper's most famous designs was the Greenbrier Hotel in White Sulphur Springs, West Virginia. During World War II, it was used as a military hospital. After the war, the Chesapeake and Ohio Railroad repurchased the property—and Dorothy Draper was retained to decorate the entire resort. She designed everything from matchbook covers to menus to staff uniforms. Draper transformed the Greenbrier in sixteen months. "Draperizing" more than six hundred guest rooms and all the public areas took forty-five thousand yards of fabric, fifteen thousand rolls of wallpaper, and forty thousand gallons of paint. In payment for her work at the Greenbrier, Draper picked up the highest fee ever paid a decorator. The $4.2 million renovation was unveiled at a house party featuring such society guests as the duke and duchess of Windsor and Bing Crosby.

At the Greenbrier, most of the public rooms were given different themes. For example, one was a pink ballroom so that the ladies of that era's faces would appear to be blushing. In the blue room next door, there were busts of United States presidents' heads. Draper thought that some of the presidents were not attractive enough and modified their busts to appear more handsome. Dorothy was the head designer of the hotel until the 1960s when she passed the job off to her mentee, Carleton Varney. By 1963, Varney, who succeeded Dorothy Draper as the president of the firm, had taken over the job of maintaining and subtly changing the décor of the Greenbrier. Since then, there have been many changes to the Greenbrier, such as the hidden vault built for emergency use by the United States Congress during the Cold War.

In the early 1950s, Packard hired Draper to harmonize the colors and fabrics of their automobile interiors. Draper's 1954 concept for the cafeteria at New York's Metropolitan Museum of Art, dubbed the Dorotheum, featured birdcage chandeliers and skylighted canopy.

In 1939, she published *Decorating is Fun!*, a design manual that was also a self-help book. As bluntly as it set out the rules of scale and symmetry, the book also took the nervous housewife by the shoulders and gave her a good shake. "If it looks right, it is right." "Don't be a slave to tradition or to your mother-in-law's taste." "Paint the ceiling, hang your own curtains, and fill the space with what you love." "The first rule of decorating, she wrote in all caps, was "courage," followed by color, balance, "smart accessories," and comfort.

Dorothy Draper was no modernist of the austere European school, but she did prize light and brightness—practicality and fun—over stifling formality. She also recognized that her reader might, like herself, be a single woman rather than a wife and mother, and she might have nobody to help her hang her curtains. Briskly, DD encouraged her to get up the ladder herself. Far better to live with the disapproval of a stuffy relative than the oppression of a dark and cluttered home. And throwing it open to others was essential! Two years later, as the country was sliding into war, Draper published her follow-up, *Entertaining is Fun!*

In May 2006, the Museum of the City of New York held an exhibition of Draper's work, curated by Donald Albrecht and designed by the Manhattan studio Pure+Applied, called "The High Style of Dorothy Draper."

> Taking an eighteenth-century chair normally done in wood and making it in clear plastic is a Dorothy Draper kind of thing. And she is a fascinating person. All of her tips must have been really great for housewives in the fifties. To have this woman telling them, "Don't be afraid! Paint the door green!"

Draper-designed furniture was lent by the Greenbrier Hotel and the Arrowhead Springs resort. A nine-foot white "birdcage" chandelier that Draper designed for the Metropolitan Museum of Art's Dorotheum café was also on display.

From December 2006 through July 2007, the Women's Museum in Dallas hosted "In the Pink: The Legendary Life of Dorothy Draper." It featured archival photographs of Draper's work from the Stoneleigh Hotel and the St. Anthony Hotel. The exhibition was designed by Pure+Applied of New York. The exhibition then moved to the Museum of Art in Fort Lauderdale from February through June 2008.

Her 1941 book, *Entertaining is Fun! How to Be a Popular Hostess*, was reissued in 2004. It had a hot-pink, polka-dotted cover and was a best-seller. Her pronouncements were legendary. She said, "The color of your front door announces your personality to the world."

Much of her work survives today in the lobbies of apartment buildings, the Carlyle Hotel and the Hampshire House in New York, and the Greenbrier in White Sulphur Springs, West Virginia.

# Chapter 15

## Morris Lapidus

Morris Lapidus (1902–2001) was a famous and successful architect, primarily known for his neo-baroque "Miami Modern" hotels constructed in the 1950s and 1960s, which have since come to define that era's resort-hotel style—synonymous with Miami and Miami Beach.

A Russian immigrant raised in New York, Lapidus designed more than a thousand buildings during a career spanning more than fifty years, much of it spent as an outsider to the American architectural establishment.

Born in Odessa in the Russian Empire (now the Ukraine), his Orthodox Jewish family fled Russian pogroms to New York when he was an infant. He attended Boys High School in Brooklyn, New York University, and the Columbia University School of Architecture, graduating in 1927. Two years later, he married his Brooklyn sweetheart, Beatrice Perlman, who died in 1992. He is survived by his sons, Richard L., a lawyer in Florida, and Alan H., an architect in the New York area; three grandchildren; and three great-grandchildren.

In his autobiography, *Too Much Is Never Enough* (Rizzoli, 1994), Mr. Lapidus traced his populist style to a childhood influence—his first vision as a Russian immigrant to Coney Island's Luna Park. It was, he said, the first time he felt "an emotional surge" about architecture:

> I was standing on the elevated platform just as dusk was falling and the lights were on. To me it was the most beautiful sight I'd seen. Of course, I knew it was hanky-pank, a circus and showmanship. But to a child of six it was all the wonders of the world. I never outgrew it.

At Columbia University, he planned on becoming a stage designer, but he began his career instead in retail design, pioneering the use of bright colors, lights, and sweeping curvilinear forms to sell merchandise.

He developed an ability to make money while many other architects were searching for work. During these years, working for several firms and later for himself, he supervised the construction of more than five hundred stores, storefronts, and showrooms for Lerner, Bond's, and Howard Clothes and shoe chains such as Florsheim, Baker, and A. S. Beck.

"I put merchandise in the open where customer could go over and touch it," Mr. Lapidus told Daniel F. Cuff in *The New York Times* in 1981. "Before that, the customer needed a salesman to get the items out for him. There were counters and heavy cabinets. 'Let's open it all up,' I said."

He worked for twenty years before designing a building. His connection with A. S. Beck led to his big break:

> A company architect had a friend in the hotel business in Florida who didn't like what the local architect was doing. My friend told him about me, about my innovative ideas, and I met with him. What experience did I have in hotels? he asked. "I have none," I told him.
>
> But I gave him my theories. Get rid of corners. Use sweeping lines. Use light to create unusual effects. Use plenty of color. Try to get drama. Keep changing the floor levels. Keep people moving and excited at all times.

The Florida hotel man, Ben Novack, hired Mr. Lapidus as associate architect of the Sans Souci Hotel. That led to half a dozen jobs in Miami Beach as an associate architect, including work for the Nautilus, the Algiers, and the Biltmore Terrace.

> When Ben Novack announced that he was building the Fontainebleau, it appeared in the New York papers that I was to be the architect. But when I called him, he said I wasn't chosen, that I never did a whole hotel and that he just needed a name at the time. It took me a year to convince him. I moved heaven and earth to get that job. "If there's one thing I'm going to do," I told myself, "I'm going to do the Fontainebleau."
>
> "And I got it. My first building after twenty years. I did everything—the logos, bellhop uniforms. It

was the chance of a lifetime. It brought me instant success. A few years later, I wouldn't touch a shop."

At the Eden Roc in 1955, to satisfy the developer Harry Mufson, Mr. Lapidus had a copy made of the Winged Victory of Samothrace. When the statue was uncrated, however, Mufson was outraged. "Where's the head?" he demanded. "For ten grand, I want a head!"

Fred Trump, the New York builder and father of Donald, admired Mr. Lapidus's work:

> He liked what I did at Sans Souci. He said, "I want you to do a lobby in an apartment house in Queens. Name any fee you like. You're my architect, design everything."

The building, the Edgerton, was in Jamaica Estates, Queens. Mr. Lapidus did the entranceway and lobby and then did several other projects for the Trump Organization and for many other clients, including the Trump Village, Cadman Plaza, and Presidential Towers apartments in New York; resort hotels in Jamaica, Switzerland, and Aruba; and stores; hospitals; office buildings; and synagogues (Temple Share Zion in Brooklyn).

In 1952, Lapidus landed the job of designing the largest luxury hotel in Miami Beach, the Fontainebleau Hotel, which was a 1,200-room hotel built by Ben Novack on the former Firestone estate—and perhaps the most famous hotel in the world.

The Lapidus style was idiosyncratic and immediately recognizable, derived as it was from the attention-getting techniques of commercial store design: sweeping curves, theatrically backlit floating ceilings, beanpoles, and the ameboid shapes that he called "woggles," "cheeseholes," and painter's palette shapes. His many smaller projects gave Miami Beach's Collins Avenue its style, anticipating postmodernism. Beyond visual style, there was some degree of functionalism at work. His curving walls caught the prevailing ocean breezes in the era before central air-conditioning, and the sequence of his interior spaces was the result of careful attention to user experience. Lapidus had heard complaints of endless featureless hotel corridors, and when possible, he would curve his hallways to avoid the effect.

The 560-room Fontainebleau was built on the site of the Harvey Firestone estate and defined the new Gold Coast of Miami Beach. The hotel provided locations for the 1960 Jerry Lewis film *The Bellboy*, a success for both Lewis and Lapidus, and the James Bond thriller *Goldfinger* (1964). Its most famous feature is the "Staircase to Nowhere" (formally called the "floating staircase"), which merely led to a mezzanine-level coat check and ladies' powder-room, but it offered the opportunity to make a glittering descent into the hotel lobby. Critics used words like splashy, colossal, gaudy, and opulent.

The Fontainebleau was once called "the nation's grossest national product." The architecture critic of the *New York Times*, Ada Louise Huxtable, wrote in 1970 that a purple-and-gold Lapidus-designed bellhop uniform at the Americana Hotel of Bal Harbour hit the eye "like an exploding gilded eggplant." The Americana of Bal Harbour was designed by Morris Lapidus after he completed the Fontainebleau, the Eden Roc, and the Sans Souci hotels.

Lapidus designed the spectacular Americana Hotel with a large glass-enclosed terrarium in the center of the lobby filled with orchids and rare plants. It functioned as a miniature rain forest, complete with periodic rain showers and artistic moonlight fixtures.

The hotel described its Bal Masque Supper Club as follows:

> The Bal Masque Supper Club is one of Florida's most fabulous nightclubs, daringly original, tremendous in scope! This is the setting for spectacular shows, featuring the top entertainers of the world, and leading orchestras. Six three-dimensional murals— shown on facing page—depict the celebrated carnival scenes of the Americas ... each mural authentic as to the costumes and musical instruments of the country it represents! Fashioned by famous Anton Refregier of wood veneer, and welded steel and bronze rods, these murals are detached from the walls; the figures actually float in space, and glow when the room is darkened for a show. The spectacular Bal Masque Room and the Medallion Room together, when the soundproof wall is removed, become the Grand Ballroom of the Americana ... scene of the most exciting events of the season!

Not content with working just with an exterior shell, Mr. Lapidus also designed the interior decorations to ensure continuity of his original concept of the hotel. Lapidus said that the Americana was "more dedicated to the spirit of play than any hotel I have ever created."

The extraordinary design effort that went into the Americana of Bal Harbour is best described by a listing of the often-overlooked artists who Lapidus hired:

- Mariana Von Allesch was born in Bavaria, the daughter of a baroness and an officer of the Imperial Army. She devoted her time to the arts and crafts, studying under European masters. Her first exhibition of blown glass in 1922 won her immediate fame. In the Americana, Miss Von Allesch did the room and lobby lamps and the door escutcheons.

- William Bowie, a native of Ohio, moved to New York to seek artistic acclaim, but he soon became dissatisfied with conventional artistic media. Always on the lookout for new media, Bowie's early mosaics were constructed of leather scraps and cellulose sponges that he used to form patterns after dyeing them various colors. His sponge mosaics were located in the Americana lobby and in the Lanai suites.

- Herman Brockdorf was born in Copenhagen, Denmark, came to the United States in 1929, and exhibited throughout the nation, winning numerous national awards. Two of his paintings were selected by the National Gallery, London, and the Glasgow Museum of Art. His art has found wide acceptance, and he was recognized as one of Florida's outstanding artists. The stone columns in the Americana lobby were his work.

- Robert Cook was born in Boston in 1921, and he studied sculpture there under George Demetrios. After serving in a model-making section of the army during World War II, he attended the Academie des Beaux Arts in Paris. He received grants by the Tiffany Foundation, the American Academy, and the National Institute of Arts and Letters—and a Fulbright commission. Cook's sculpture was modeled in a heavy beeswax with a hot soldering iron. This resulted in a delicacy not available through other techniques. Others of his works were in wood and bronze, such as "Rodeo," which was the Americana's showpiece.

- Audrey Corwin was a Florida artist known for her over-life-sized monument portraits for the University of Miami and for the bust of George Washington Carver in the State National Park in Diamond, Missouri. The miniature mountain in the Americana terrarium was originally sculpted in model size by Miss Corwin.

- Elmo Gideon was a native of Kansas who studied at the Chicago Academy of Fine Arts. Awards in the American Artist Professional League included first prize, 1951; best overall award, 1955; and grand national finalist, 1956. The Caribbean suite figures and guest room oil paintings were his work.

- Charles R. Jacobson was one of the nation's most famous nonobjective painters. He had been a resident of Miami since 1944, and he spent much of his time in the Caribbean and Mexico. The copper column panels in the lobby were the work of Mr. Jacobson.

- Anton Refregier, one of America's best-known contemporary artists, was a New Yorker whose paintings are in collections from coast to coast. His work has been exhibited in all the principal national shows, and he has been the recipient of numerous awards. A lecturer and author in addition to his artistic talents, Refregier taught art throughout the nation. His principal medium has been ceramic tile murals. At the Americana, Mr. Refregier did the theme mosaic figures in the lobby and the Bal Masque carnival murals.

- James Seeman, a muralist and engineering designer, came to the United States in 1938 from his native Vienna and opened his first studio in New York at the war's end. Mr. Seeman designed the American's original wallpapers, tile panels, elevator foyer tile hangings, Carioca Room decorations, and the grand stairway wall décor.

Although the *New York Times* called it a "bizarre design," the Americana of Bal Harbour was a huge success.

# The Summit Hotel, New York, New York

In 1961, the twenty-one-story Summit Hotel, designed by architect Morris Lapidus, was the first new transient hotel built in Manhattan in thirty years. Ambassador Carlos P. Rormulo of the Philippines presided at the dedication, which was attended by Noel Coward and Judy Garland. June Platt, Britain's coffee queen, helped open the Mayan-themed Casa del Café coffee shop, and a taste of Argentina was featured in the Gaucho Room, where the walls were covered in cowhide, lamp fixtures were shaped like steer skulls, and the ceiling was ornamented with cattle brands.

With its wavy green exterior, the building seemed to be outside the limits of New York architectural design. Flamboyant and colorful, its curving façade coated in seafoam-colored brick was described by Ada Louise Huxtable, architectural critic of the *New York Times,* as "being too far from the beach."

In describing the elongated S-shaped design for the Summit, architect Morris Lapidus said that more rooms could be built along a serpentine layout than a straight corridor. As to why he chose blue and green for the façade, he said,

> Because there is too little color in New York City. Color is uplifting and brightness provides gaiety, a sense of anticipation; and emotional element which I feel is necessary to the success of any hotel design. I have many times watched a large segment of the public respond naturally and with obvious pleasure to the theory behind a particular design of mine. Lack of architectural knowledge apparently presents no bar to what I call man's instinctive capacity for pleasure in his surroundings.

Disclosure: In 1963, I was appointed the general manager of the Summit Hotel, and I served there for two and a half years.

## The Americana of New York

In 1962, Morris Lapidus designed the two-thousand room Americana Hotel on Seventh Avenue and Fifty-Third Street. It was the first hotel with more than a thousand rooms to be built in New York since the Waldorf-Astoria in 1931. With fifty-one floors, it was acclaimed for many years as the tallest hotel in the world. It was built, along with the New York Hilton facing Sixth Avenue on the next block, to serve the large numbers that the 1964 New York World's Fair would bring.

The Americana of New York had a nightclub, "the Royal Box," which hosted performances by Ella Fitzgerald, Pearl Bailey, Duke Ellington, Julie London, Peggy Lee, Sonny and Cher, Leslie Uggams, B. B. King, Wayne Newton, and Liberace, among many other stars.

On July 21, 1972, American Airlines leased the Americana of New York as well as the City Squire Motor Inn across the street, the Americanas of Miami Beach and San Juan, Puerto Rico for thirty years. They merged these hotels with their Sky Chefs Hotels under the Americana Hotels brand.

In 1979, the Americana of New York and the City Squire were sold to Sheraton Hotels and the Equitable Life Assurance Society, and in 2013, it was renamed the Sheraton New York Times Square Hotel.

Disclosure: In 1962, I was hired as the resident manager of the Americana of New York. I lived in a one-bedroom suite on the forty-fifth floor and reported to Tom Troy, the general manager who had worked for and learned the hotel business from Ellsworth Statler.

By June 1961, the Tisches began to implement their expansion plan to build two motor hotels, an apartment hotel, and a movie house, all in Manhattan, and a 450-room Americana Hotel in San Juan, Puerto Rico.

Lapidus described his theory of design as follows:

> I wanted people to feel something. If two people were walking by one of my buildings and one said to the other, "Did you notice that building?" and the other said, "What building?" I've failed. But if he looks at it and says, "Oh my god" or "That monstrosity," I was glad. Because he noticed me."

Lapidus described his formula for success in the hotel business:

> My whole success is I've always been designing for people, first because I wanted to sell them merchandise. Then when I got into hotels, I had to rethink, what am I selling now? You're selling a good time.

Mr. Lapidus often said that he could not abide a straight line. "A staircase isn't a staircase unless it's curved," he said. And he expounded upon what he called his moth theory: that people are attracted to light.

Despite his theory, he often acknowledged that he was not really an innovator. "I wasn't the founder of style. I'm just an architect who happened to be carried away by his emotions."

He also designed one hundred condominiums in Florida and lived his later years in Miami Beach in a building he designed in the 1960s. The apartment overlooked Biscayne Bay and was filled with Lucite, gold, and mother-of-pearl.

During the period before his death, Lapidus's style came back into focus. It began with designing upbeat restaurants on Miami Beach and the Lincoln Road Mall. Lapidus was also honored by the Society of Architectural Historians at a convention held at the Eden Roc Hotel in 1998. In 2000, the Smithsonian's Cooper-Hewitt National Design Museum honored Lapidus as an "American original" for his lifetime of work. Lapidus said, "I never thought I would live to see the day when, suddenly, magazines are writing about me, newspapers are writing about me."

Ben Novack Sr. had a dream of building the world's greatest hotel in Miami Beach. During World War II, the US Army requisitioned more than 180 hotels and one hundred apartment buildings in Miami Beach. As the owner of several hotels, Novack's contracts with the Army made him rich. In 1954, Novack built the Fontainebleau Hotel on an estate purchased from the heirs of the Firestone family for $16 million, which made it one of the most expensive of its time.

Novack hired the Russian-born American architect Morris Lapidus at a bargain price to design the Fontainebleau. When it opened in 1954, critics lambasted the Lapidus designs, calling his architecture "pornography of architecture" and "boarding house baroque."

The Fontainebleau was the height of excess with woggles and cheeseholes and a curved design that provided more guest rooms with ocean views. Novack and Lapidus disagreed on many issues from the name to the design of the hotel. Despite the disagreements, the Fontainebleau Hotel opened on December 20, 1954, with pomp and ceremony and a $50-a-plate opening party for 1,600 guests. The hotel's La Ronde Room opened on Christmas Eve with Vaughn Monroe and his orchestra. In subsequent shows, the LaRonde hosted Frank Sinatra, Dean Martin and Jerry Lewis, Liberace, Elvis Presley, and other famous entertainers. The James Bond movie *Goldfinger* used the hotel as its background. The Fontainebleau became and, to this day, remains Miami Beach's most famous hotel. It was so well recognized that there was no sign at the front of the hotel until the 1970s.

Morris Lapidus's relationship with Novack ended when he agreed to design the Eden Roc Hotel for Harry Mufson immediately north of the Fontainebleau. The Eden Roc was new and beautiful when it opened in 1955 and has remained one of the Miami Beach jewels.

Ben Novack Sr. died at seventy-eight years of age in 1985. He had operated the Fontainebleau Hotel for twenty-four years—from the time it was built until it was sold in 1978. Ben's son, Ben Jr., and his mother, eighty-six-year-old Bernice, were murdered in 2009. Ben Jr.'s wife, Narcy, and her brother were sentenced to life imprisonment for hiring hit men to kill Ben Jr. and Bernice.

# BIBLIOGRAPHY

Alpern, Andrew. *The New York Apartment Houses of Rosario Candela and James Carpenter.* Acanthus Press: New York, 2001.

Alpern, Andrew. *Apartments for the Affluent: A Historical Survey of Buildings in New York.* McGraw-Hill, 1975.

Baker, Paul R. *Stanny: The Gilded Life of Stanford White.* New York: Free Press, 1989.

Broderick, Mosette. *Triumvirate: McKim, Mead, and White: Art, Architecture, Scandal, and Class in America's Gilded Age.* Alfred A. Knopf. 2010.

Broderick, Mosette and William Shopsin. *The Villard Houses: Life Story of a Landmark.* New York: Viking Press, 1980.

Cigliano, Jan and Sarah Landau. *The Grand American Avenue, 1850–1920.* San Francisco: Pomegranate Artbooks, 1994.

Craven, Wayne. *Stanford White: Decorator in Opulence and Dealer in Antiquities.* New York: Columbia University Press, 2005.

Cromley, Elizabeth. *Alone Together: A History of New York's Early Apartments.* Ithaca: Cornell University Press, 1990.

Denby, Elaine. *Grand Hotels: Reality and Illusion: An Architectural and Social History.* Reaktion Books Ltd., 1998.

Dorsey, Leslie and Janice Devine. *Fare Thee Well.* New York: Grosset and Dunlap, 1968

Dryfhout, John H. *The Work of Augustus Saint-Gaudens.* Hanover, NH, and London: University Press of New England, 1982.

Filler, Martin. *Makers of Modern Architecture.* Volume I, II, III; *New York Review of Books*, 2018.

Groth, Paul. *Living Downtown: The History of Residential Hotels in the United States.* University of California Press, Berkeley, California, 1994.

Hayden, Dolores. *The Grand Domestic Revolution: A History of Feminist Designs for American Homes, Neighborhoods, and Cities.* Cambridge: MIT Press, 1981.

Hepburn, Andrew. *Great Resorts of North America.* Garden City, New York: Doubleday and Co., 1965.

Hitchcock, Henry-Russell. *The Architecture of H. H. Richardson and His Times.* Rev. ed. Cambridge, Massachusetts: MIT Press, 1966.

Kozol, Jonathan. *Rachel and Her Children: Homeless Families in America.* New York: Crown Publishers, 1988.

Kramer, J.J. *The Last of the Grand Hotels.* Van Nostrand Reinhold Company Ltd. 1978.

Lewis, Oscar, and Carroll D. Hall. *Bonanza Inn: America's First Luxury Hotel.* New York: Alfred A. Knopf, 1939.

Lewis, Sinclair. *Work of Art.* Garden City, New York: Doubleday, Doran and Company, 1935.

Limerick, Jeffrey, Nancy Ferguson, Richard Oliver. *America's Grand Resort Hotels.* Pantheon Books, 1979.

McGinty, Brian. *The Palace Inns: A Connoisseur's Guide to Historic American Hotels.* Stackpole Books, Harrisburg, Pennsylvania, 1978.

Mostafavi, Mohsen, ed. *Portman's America and Other Speculations.* Harvard University Graduate School of Design; Lars Müller Publishers, 2017.

Moudon, Anne Vernez. *Built for Change: Neighborhood Architecture in San Francisco.* Cambridge: MIT Press, 1986.

Plunz, Richard. *A History of Housing in New York City: Dwelling Type and Social Change in the American Metropolis.* New York: Columbia University Press, 1990.

Ruttenbaum, Steven. *Mansions in the Clouds: The Skyscraper Palazzi of Emery Roth.* Balsam Press, Inc., 1986.

Saliga, Pauline A., ed. *The Sky's the Limit: A Century of Chicago Skyscrapers.* New York: Rizzoli, 1990.

Sandoval-Strausz, A.K., *Hotel. An American History.* Yale University Press, 2007.

Sexton, Randolph Williams. *American Apartment Houses, Hotels, and Apartment Hotels of Today.* New York: Architectural Book Publishing Co., 1929.

Stamper, John W. *Chicago's North Michigan Avenue; Planning and Development, 1900–1930.* Chicago: University of Chicago Press, 1991.

Stern, Robert A.M. Gregory Gilmartin and Thomas Mellins. *New York 1930: Architecture and Urbanism between the Two World Wars.* New York: Rizzoli, 1987.

# INDEX

**Y**

YMCA, xi, 75, 100, 103,119-120, 130

**Z**

Zeckendorf, William, 44, 51, 81
Zig Zag, 182
Zweig, Stefan, 88